Classroom Management

A Practical Approach for Primary and Secondary Teachers

Harry Ayers and Francesca Gray

David Fulton Publishers
London

David Fulton Publishers Ltd
The Chiswick Centre, 414 Chiswick High Road, London W4 5TF
www.fultonpublishers.co.uk

First published in Great Britain in 1998 by David Fulton Publishers

Note: The rights of Harry Ayers and Francesca Gray to be identified as the
authors of this work have been asserted by them in accordance with the
Copyright, Designs and Patents Act 1988.

David Fulton Publishers is a division of Granada Learning Limited, part of
Granada plc.

British Library Cataloguing in Publication Data
A catalogue record for this book is available from the British Library.

ISBN 1-85346-510-0

Typeset by Helen Skelton, London
Printed and bound in Great Britain

Contents

Preface

This book is designed to meet the basic classroom management needs of teachers in all phases and types of educational institution.

It introduces teachers to the main theoretical approaches to classroom management of learning and behaviour along with their practical applications. In addition, the book considers the needs of particular categories of pupils and other issues that impact on classroom management.

Last but not least it provides a range of photocopiable forms that will enable teachers to assess, monitor and analyse their management of learning and behaviour in the classroom.

Harry Ayers and Francesca Gray
January 1998

Chapter 1

Introduction to classroom management

Effective teaching and class assessment

Teachers need to consider general points about the bases of effective teaching and the processes of assessment of their pupils in relation to classroom management.

Effective teaching

Teachers are recommended to:

- ensure that they are **knowledgeable about their curriculum area**, have relevant teaching skills, engage in self-appraisal, are empathic and equipped with managerial techniques;

- ensure their lessons are **prepared and planned in terms of lesson aims, objectives, content, materials and presentation** and are also monitored and evaluated (both in summative and formative terms);

- **display effective teaching qualities** which include Kounin's 'withitness' (vigilance (1977)), 'overlapping' (simultaneous focus on several tasks), 'smoothness' (avoiding abrupt transitions) and 'momentum' (avoiding a pace that is too slow or too fast);

- ensure that **pupils are actually engaged in the learning process**, i.e. pupils should be attentive, receptive and feel that the learning is appropriate;

- ensure that there is a **balance between exposition and set tasks**;

- encourage **discovery and experiential learning** (use of AVA, role-play, drama and visits), investigations and problem-solving activities;

- use a balance of **direct** (teacher-structured and organised) and **indirect instruction** (pupil exercises initiative and responsibility);

- use **explanations** that are clear, segmented, succinct, interesting, understandable and that elicit feedback;

- use '**advanced organisers**' and '**end of lesson reviews**' (Ausubel 1963);

- encourage pupils when appropriate to be both **intrinsically and extrinsically motivated**;

- ensure that **questioning** is appropriately targeted, is undertaken using appropriate cues, tone, prompts and pauses, allows feedback and is encouraging and sensitive;

- take account of **pupil differences** with regard to their 'ability', attainment and also underachievement, levels of motivation, gender, ethnicity and special educational needs;

- consider the **physical appearance and layout of the classroom** and arrange it so that the groupings of pupils facilitate learning, and also consider the effects of setting and streaming on pupils;

- consider the **effects of class size** on learning and the best use of support staff;

- use **appropriately individualised learning programmes** (project work, computer-assisted learning and structured work schemes), small-group work ('collaborative working' or 'peer-group tutoring' in terms of achieving specific tasks or exploration of issues) and whole-class teaching.

Teachers need to be familiar with these recommendations as they can be seen as providing the necessary conditions or bases for teachers to develop effective classroom management. Reduction in pupil misbehaviour can be achieved by implementing these recommendations before considering further specific measures.

Assessment

Assessment is a process that is undertaken with regard to learning and behaviour. It is either **criterion** or **norm-referenced** or a mixture of both.

There are various different types of assessment, some of which teachers will not be able to use, but they may come across them in medical, psychiatric or psychological reports. These are **neuropsychological**, **psychiatric** and **psychological** assessments.

- **Neuropsychological assessment** uses a combination of brain imaging and tests to detect in children neurological lesions or abnormalities that bring about or contribute to behavioural or emotional problems.

- **Psychiatric assessment** uses standardised classification systems to diagnose mental or psychiatric disorders. Usually a diagnostic manual is used – either DSM IV or ICD 10. Children are then diagnosed as having a particular disorder, e.g. attention deficit/hyperactivity disorder (ADHD), conduct disorder or separation anxiety disorder. This type of assessment is undertaken through clinical interviews.

- **Psychological assessment** may use standardised intelligence, reading and personality tests, observation, interviews and rating scales to assess the behaviour and learning of children.

Teachers need to assess the interactions between themselves and their pupils and the interactions between pupils in their classrooms. It is also necessary to assess how the classroom environment, referral and pastoral systems are impacting on their classrooms. The teacher can use **behavioural, cognitive** and **ecosystemic** types of assessment, and a general assessment should be undertaken first which will include basic facts about the pupils and the class as a whole including reading ages and National Curriculum levels.

- The aim of **behavioural assessment** is to describe the specific, overt and observable learning and behaviour of pupils in the class and the antecedents and consequences of behaviours. This can be achieved by using formal and informal observation and the use of behaviour checklists. The ABC, or functional analysis, enables teachers to assess the antecedents and consequences of a given behaviour or the predisposing, precipitating and perpetuating factors that influence behaviour.

- The aim of **cognitive assessment** is to describe the attitudes and beliefs of pupils towards school, learning, teachers and other pupils. This can be achieved by using structured questionnaires and sociometry.

- The aim of **ecosystemic assessment** is to describe interactions between teachers and pupils. This can be undertaken through questionnaires that focus on teacher and pupil perceptions of their classroom interactions.

Assessment is undertaken to arrive at a formulation, that is, a statement of why learning and behavioural problems are occurring and why they are continuing.

- A **behavioural formulation** concentrates on the ways in which pupils' learning and behaviours are being reinforced and maintained through environmental – in this case classroom – contingencies.

- A **cognitive formulation** will focus on the ways in which pupils' learning and behaviours are affected by the attitudes and beliefs they hold about themselves, each other and their teachers. Teachers will need to survey their pupils' attitudes and expectations with regard to learning and behaviour.

- An **ecosystemic formulation** will focus on the cycle of positive or negative interactions between teachers and pupils and how these influence learning and behaviour. This requires teachers to engage in self-analyses about their interactions with pupils and to find out from pupils their interpretations of those interactions.

Assessment	Behavioural	Cognitive	Ecosystemic
	Description of specific, overt and observable behaviour.	Description of beliefs, attitudes and expectations.	Description of positive and negative interactions.

Specifics of classroom management

Task analysis

It is helpful for teachers to undertake task analyses, that is, to plan programmes for pupils that are broken down into their component parts, and that state instructional objectives and skills required of their pupils. The programme should state clear targets, identify the skills required from simple to complex, identify those already available and then proceed, teaching simple skills first.

Expectations

It is also useful for teachers to undertake an analysis of their expectations and those of their pupils.

Teachers develop expectations of their pupils which have a positive or negative impact on their behaviour and/or learning. As indicated in Rosenthal and Jacobsen's (1968) research, teachers' expectations may lead to a self-fulfilling prophecy. Particular aspects of pupils – such as their gender, special educational needs and ethnicity – can influence teachers' expectations.

Pupils' negative as well as positive expectations should be identified by teachers. These expectations can relate to work, teachers and their peers. Pupils may expect that they will be unable to cope with the work set by teachers or that they will not be able to get on with their teachers or their peers. Peers may exert positive or negative pressure on each other, facilitating or obstructing learning. An anti-learning or behaviourally deviant classroom subculture may develop.

Parental expectations can also influence their children's behaviour and learning. Parents may have unrealistically high or low expectations of their children's learning ability, leading their children to feel either under- or overconfident. Teachers should attempt to modify or change parental expectations where necessary.

Planning and teaching

Teachers should develop and implement classroom rules and lesson plans. Classroom rules need to be minimal, positive and have consequences attached, and should be discussed with pupils prior to implementation. Teacher behavioural and learning expectations should be clearly established.

Pupils should be seated so that they can see clearly what the teacher is presenting, so the teacher can see them clearly and so the teacher has easy access to the class. Teaching materials should also be easily accessible.

Pupils should be arranged into small or large groups according to the type of learning required. Small groups are useful for teaching basic skills, particularly to pupils with learning difficulties, as they enable more pupil participation, while large-group teaching is more appropriate for teaching subject content than specific skills.

Where a pupil has learning difficulties with a basic skill teachers should, where possible, provide one-to-one teaching. Peer tutoring is another method of providing this more intensive help to pupils within the classroom. Two pupils are paired in a tutor–tutee arrangement, the aim being to increase the learning but also in some cases the behaviour of the tutee. In order for peer tutoring to be effective, targets and skills should be identified, materials selected, timetables drawn up, procedures established, tutors and tutees trained and progress evaluated.

Cooperative learning involves pupils working together in small groups. This approach places the emphasis on identifying team targets and team success through pupils becoming responsible for the learning of others in the group as well as for their own learning. In order for cooperative learning to be effective, pupils in the group should have a spread of attainments.

Scheduling activities is where teachers plan activities considering such factors as length of tasks, timing of tasks, variety of tasks, difficulty of tasks, preferred and non-preferred tasks, and whether tasks can be completed within lesson time. Activities and teaching materials selected should be differentiated according to the range of ability levels within the class.

Factors that contribute to effective teaching				
Organisation	Objectives and aims	Methods	Materials	Assessment
Advanced organisers	Long- and short-term objectives	Expository teaching – advanced organisers	Textbooks	Criterion or norm-referenced
Scaffolding	SMART targets	Scaffolding	Worksheets	Written tests
Audio-visual			Question-naires	Essays
Direct instruction and explan-ation	Acquisition and perform-ance of knowledge and skills	Discovery learning	Tests	Multiple-choice
Question and answer	Timing and pace	Reinforce-ment	Audio-visual	Verbal questioning and feedback
Cueing and feedback	High expectations	Modelling	Information technology	Demonstra-tion
Discussion	IEPs	Audio-visual	Differentia-ted by task and outcome	Observation
Positive reinforce-ment		Question and answer		Pupil self-assessment
Modelling		Cueing and feedback		Marking effects
Research		Discussion		SATs
		Action research		NC levels

Specific approaches to teaching and learning

The behavioural or operant approach

The behavioural or operant approach to teaching exemplified by Skinner (1953) focuses on changing the antecedents and consequences of both behaviour and learning. This approach emphasises techniques such as **cueing** (providing an antecedent stimulus), **prompting** (giving another cue after the first) and **reinforcement of learning** (rewarding an appropriate response). A skill or behaviour can be **shaped** by reinforcing successive approximations to the target skill or behaviour. This requires a **task analysis** that breaks down the learning process into small steps.

The cognitive approach

The cognitive approach is exemplified by Bruner, Goodknow and Austin's (1956) and Ausubel's (1963) models of learning and teaching.

Bruner focuses on understanding the structure of a subject and the value of **active learning** and **inductive reasoning**. Teachers should present problems to their pupils so that their pupils actively explore and discover for themselves the interconnections between subject concepts. Bruner advocates **guided discovery** for primary and secondary pupils: the teacher provides interesting problems and encourages pupils to generate hypotheses and test solutions. Discovery learning is not recommended for pupils of lower ability as it presupposes adequate problem-solving skills.

Ausubel focuses on the value of the teacher's direct presentation of knowledge to pupils but proposes that learning should proceed deductively. He advocates **expository teaching** where teachers organise their material in a way that can be assimilated by their pupils, and proposes **advance organisers** that provide structures for the acquisition of new knowledge. They remind pupils of pre-existing knowledge (comparative organisers) or impart knowledge that is necessary for assimilating new concepts (expository organisers).

The social learning approach

The social learning approach, exemplified by Bandura (1986), focuses on the effects of imitation and modelling on learning. **Observational learning** occurs when pupils copy the behaviours of others. This can happen through **vicarious reinforcement** where pupils see other pupils being rewarded for the performance of certain skills or behaviours or without reinforcement where pupils are already motivated to want to learn a skill or behaviour. **Modelling** occurs where teachers demonstrate to their pupils a particular skill or behaviour. Observational learning depends for its effectiveness on four factors: attention, retention, production and motivation, and reinforcement. Teachers should prepare lessons that encourage their pupils to pay attention, that increase retention and production of knowledge and skills through feedback, rehearsal and practice, and that motivate pupils through reinforcement.

Chapter 2

The concepts of class and group dynamics

Class and group dynamics

A class is composed of a variety of individual pupils who may differ according to a number of characteristics, for example ability, attainment, age, gender, ethnicity and personality. This makes it very difficult – or impossible – to generalise about classes as a whole. The varying composition of classes has to be carefully considered when proposing classroom management strategies or interventions.

The kinds of interactions between teachers and pupils will to a great extent determine learning and behaviour in the classroom. Classes are composed of groups that interact with each other positively and negatively and of individual pupils who also interact positively and negatively with each other.

The attitudes of pupils towards each other are often major determinants of the learning and behavioural ethos of the classroom. Pupils can sometimes find the process of adapting to each other's personalities difficult. This can be reflective of a lack of social or learning skills or of the unwillingness of pupils to use their social skills when they feel that they are in the right. Sometimes, when a particular pupil or pupils are absent, the whole dynamic of the classroom changes, and sometimes the strategy of changing the class or form of a pupil has a positive effect on both the pupil and the class. On rare occasions where classes have manifested deeply entrenched problems, they are disaggregated and reformed in order to facilitate learning and behaviour. However, it may also be the case that a pupil is scapegoated for what is actually a whole-class or group problem.

Class dynamics can also be affected by:

- the physical environment or the context in which the class is embedded, and by the ways in which groups are arranged and structured. If left to make their own choices, pupils may form groups that are antagonistic or obstructive to both learning and behavioural outcomes;

- particular school policies – in particular, a policy of streaming classes may encourage the formation of an anti-school culture among those pupils in the lower streams;

- the teachers' attitudes and expectations – they may have positive or negative attitudes towards pupils, which are identified and internalised by those pupils (who similarly have expectations); pupils may then behave in such a way as to confirm those attitudes or expectations

- indirectly, the parents, to the extent that they are supportive or involved in the education of their children: those parents hostile to schools and teachers may encourage in their children an anti-educational bias, which adversely impacts on the classroom. Partnership with parents is important in enlisting their support in encouraging a positive ethos of learning and behaviour in the classroom.

Class dynamics

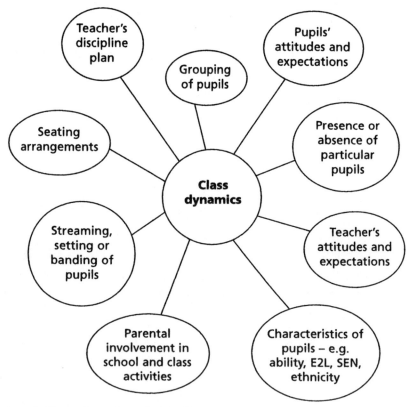

Factors influencing class dynamics

Comparative classroom management approaches

Approach	Theory	Practice
Behavioural I. Pavlov	• Classical and operant conditioning • Stimulus-response	• Systematic desensitisation • Graded and rapid exposure
B. Skinner	• Reinforcement • Contingencies • Antecedents and consequences	• Positive and negative reinforcement • Shaping, fading, extinction • Changing antecedents and consequences
Counselling C. Rogers	• Phenomenological understanding • Self-actualisation • Conditions of worth	• Facilitation of learning • Empathy, unconditional positive regard and genuineness
H. Ginott	• Congruent communication	• Sane messages
T. Gordon	• Problem ownership	• Confrontative and helping skills
B. Rogers	• Teacher–pupil communication	• Classroom discipline plan
Democratic R. Dreikurs	• Attachment • Democratic teaching	• Logical consequences • Collaboration skills • Redirection
Research-based J. Kounin	• Derived from empirical classroom observation	• Desists and 'withitness' • Momentum and smoothness • Alerting and accountability • Overlapping and challenge arousal
Cognitive A. Beck	• Information processing model • Cognitive schemas • Cognitive distortions	• Self-monitoring • Identifying, clarifying, examining beliefs • Counteract cognitive distortions
A. Ellis	• Rationalism/empiricism • Cognitive appraisal • Rational and irrational beliefs	• Logical and empirical challenging of irrational beliefs • Multimodal
A. Bandura	• Social learning • Observational learning • Self-efficacy and expectancies	• Modelling • Guided participation *Cont ...*

Ecological and ecosystemic A. Molnar and B. Lindquist	• Systems theory • Environmental factors • Recursive causality • Family therapy • Interactionism	• Environmental change • Ecosystemic techniques, e.g. reframing • Whole-school policies
Assertive discipline L. Canter and M. Canter	• Positive attention and appraisal • Effective communication	• Classroom discipline plan • Positive recognition • Consequences

Chapter 3

Theoretical approaches and their practical applications to classroom and group management

■ The counselling approach

★ **C. Rogers**
★ **H. Ginott**
★ **T. Gordon**
★ **B. Rogers**

Introduction

This approach is concerned with promoting effective communication between teachers and pupils. It is influenced by the ideas of Carl Rogers, and incorporates a phenomenological view of reality, the concept of self-actualisation, organismic valuing processes, the development of a self-concept, the need for positive regard, conditions of worth, incongruence and unconditional positive regard.

Theory

- The **phenomenological view of reality** refers to the way people perceive and interpret the world around them, e.g. how teachers and pupils perceive each other, their classes and the school.

- **Self-actualisation** refers to a process by which people strive to realise their potential for growth and development. This process is connected to **organismic valuing processes** which value positively life-enhancing experiences and value negatively life-hindering experiences. One's **concept of self** should be in harmony with one's organismic valuing experiences.

The need for **positive regard** is based on **conditions of worth**, whereby feelings of worth are influenced by what other people set out as conditions for receiving positive regard. Conditions of worth can conflict with what people value organismically and result in

incongruence, which leads to the avoidance of experience which in turn restricts growth. Being shown **unconditional positive regard** and limiting conditions of worth enable people to harness their potential for growth.

Carl Rogers (1969) sees teachers as facilitators who can bring about congruence between pupils' selves and their oganismic valuing processes. Teachers can facilitate learning by, for example, treating all their pupils as having the potential for learning, making the subject content relevant to them, encouraging them to participate and reflect on the learning process and helping them to assess their own learning.

Ginott (1971) and **Gordon** (1989) see teachers as needing to be effective communicators who should be aware of the continuous exchange of messages within the classroom, in terms of what they communicate to pupils and what pupils communicate to them.

B. Rogers (1990) highlights the need for a classroom discipline plan that emphasises the importance of communication between teachers and pupils.

Practice

Carl Rogers (1969)

Rogers states that teachers should understand the phenomenological or subjective world of their pupils, i.e. how their pupils understand and interpret teachers, other pupils and the world of the classroom. Teachers need to help develop their pupils' self-understanding, their understanding of others and their understanding of their environment. Teachers are also seen as facilitators who help foster a positive classroom ethos, who help pupils to motivate themselves and who show the personal qualities of **empathy**, warmth and **genuineness** towards their pupils. These personal qualities will in turn enable pupils to develop self-awareness, self-motivation and self-discipline. The counselling approach places little significance on the use of techniques or strategies for classroom control but instead emphasises the influence of empathy, warmth and genuineness on bringing about in pupils a self-awareness and self-discipline that reduces disruption.

Key concepts	★ Phenomenological approach
	★ Empathy
	★ Unconditional positive regard
	★ Congruence or genuineness

H. Ginott (1971)

Ginott emphasises **congruent communication**, where teachers concern themselves with pupils' situations rather than their personal qualities. They acknowledge their pupils' perceptions, experiences and feelings about their situations. Teachers should avoid deliberately or even inadvertently labelling or denigrating their pupils. They must also avoid moralising or dictating to their pupils, rather they should invite their pupils to cooperate with them in achieving their goals. Pupils should be allowed to make genuine comments without being derided or denigrated. Teachers can express anger but should direct it at the specific behaviours, not the pupil. Where teachers correct pupils they should use laconic phrases that pupils will understand, and praise should be appreciative of the particular behaviour but not evaluative of the pupils as a person. Pupils should be allowed to maintain their personal space and privacy without feeling that teachers are being intrusive or invasive. Where pupils are caught misbehaving they should be redirected to perform the appropriate behaviour for the situation. Teachers should also avoid performing the very behaviours they criticise in their pupils, and sarcasm, dictatorial approaches and punishment are best avoided as along with labelling they ultimately invite pupil resistance. Classroom management is seen by Ginott as being achieved gradually through a series of small steps.

Teachers should (congruent communication):

- send sane messages that acknowledge the feelings and situations of pupils. Correction should take the form of describing the behaviour required without denigrating the pupil. An insane message would be one where a teacher attacks the pupil personally;

- invite cooperation from their pupils by asking them what kind of behaviour they think is required in order to undertake and complete given tasks. This places the onus on pupils;

- acknowledge and show empathy for the views and feelings expressed by their pupils;

- show respect for their pupils whenever an opportunity arises;

- be genuine with their pupils and not hide their own feelings towards their pupils – including anger – as long as they do not assault their pupils' characters;

- communicate laconically or succinctly with their pupils and not preach to them but instead focus on possible solutions to the problems they present;

- give appreciative praise to their pupils for their work and effort rather than evaluative praise for their character.

Teachers should not (**incongruent communication**):

- label their pupils in a derogatory way that may lead pupils to internalise negative thinking about themselves;

- show up pupils in front of others – i.e. embarrass them or belittle them – particularly by the use of 'why' questions couched in a hostile manner;

- invade the privacy of their pupil. Pupils may wish to keep themselves to themselves and this should be respected. Intrusive questioning may end up being resented;

- make negative comments about other teachers, instead they should describe the problem and suggest alternatives;

- dwell too much on pupils' misbehaviour but instead deal with it as economically as possible;

- make sarcastic comments about their pupils – this may well provoke resentment.

Key concepts	★ Congruent communication ★ Incongruent communication

T. Gordon (1989)

Gordon argues that teachers should avoid an authoritarian or a laissez-faire approach to classroom management. Pupils should be taught self-control or self-discipline. Teachers should not rely on punishment or rewards to control their pupils, i.e. they should not be controlling. Rewards and punishments are seen as being ineffective as well as having undesirable side effects. The ownership of a particular problem behaviour should be considered first: a pupil can be seen as owning the problem that is simply and solely a problem affecting that pupil and nobody else; when the pupil's problem affects the teacher, the teacher then owns the problem. Where the pupil owns the problem, a teacher should encourage the pupil through **helping skills**; where the teacher owns the problem, **confrontative skills** are used; where neither the pupil nor the teacher own the problem, then **preventive skills** should be employed.

Confrontative skills are those where teachers:

- change the environment through enrichment, e.g. displaying pupils' work or rearranging groups;

- recognise that any negative feelings that they have towards pupils are better appraised as positive, e.g. anger towards pupils can be seen as the expression of disappointment in them;

- send I-messages whereby they inform pupils that they are upset and why they are upset, instead of you-messages that put all the blame on pupils;
- change direction if pupils react negatively to I-messages;
- on experiencing conflict adopt a no-lose conflict resolution approach. Teachers and their pupils speak about and listen to each others' grievances, attempting to avoid a win–lose situation that damages the teacher–pupil relationship.

Helping skills are those where teachers:

- use listening skills, i.e. listen carefully to pupils and the problems they present. Listening should assume the following forms:
  - 'passive listening' – where teachers listen in silence and show they are listening through non-verbal communication;
  - 'acknowledgement of responses' – where teachers respond positively to pupils by using verbal and non-verbal methods;
  - 'door opening' – where teachers encourage pupils to talk about their problems';
  - 'active listening' – where teachers listen to their pupils and help them to articulate their responses, but at the same time avoid any judgemental comments;
- circumvent communication roadblocks, i.e. where teachers unconsciously create obstacles to communication between themselves and their pupils. Twelve such roadblocks are recognised: giving orders, warning, preaching, advising, lecturing, criticising, name-calling, analysing, praising, reassuring, questioning and withdrawing. Of these twelve perhaps the ones most likely to obstruct communications are criticising and name-calling, where teachers dwell on their pupils' inadequacies or faults;
- use preventive skills in order to avoid problems occurring in the future. I-messages are used to prevent future problems by stating the kinds of behaviour required in the future without dwelling on problems that have occurred in the past. Rules should be set collaboratively between teachers and their pupils after discussion of each others' needs. Classroom management should also be achieved through pupil participation in decision making. Pupils are encouraged to use a six-stage problem-solving model: 1) identifying and defining the problem; 2) generating alternatives; 3) evaluating the alternatives; 4) decision making; 5) implementation; 6) evaluation.

Key concepts	★ Confrontative skills ★ Helping skills ★ Preventive skills

B. Rogers (1990)

B. Rogers advocates the development and use of a **classroom discipline plan** because what happens in the classroom has a significant impact on the school as a whole. Discipline is seen as being determined by such factors as the teacher's approach to discipline, the planning the teacher undertakes, the consistency with which the plan is applied and support that can be provided. Pupils are seen as preferring teachers who are assertive without being aggressive, who provide direction without coercion and who are given choices rather than warnings.

In developing their plans, teachers should:

- include rules that are perceived as fair, clear, enforceable and as being 'owned'. Rules should be specific, few, clear, fair and positive and cover interpersonal relationships, learning procedures, assistance, movement, safety and interpersonal communication;

- make it clear to pupils what the consequences are for misbehaviour and have strategies available for specific kinds of misbehaviour;

- reflect on the verbal and non-verbal communication they use with their pupils, e.g. tone of voice and body language;

- use interventions that start with the least intrusive, e.g. ignoring misbehaviour, and then where the situation warrants it proceed to the most intrusive, e.g. time out;

- place an emphasis on building positive relationships and the avoidance of grudges;

- make sure they have exit strategies for when pupils need to be removed from the classroom;

- distinguish between a short-term issue where they can use an immediate response to misbehaviour, e.g. a reprimand, and a long-term issue where they need to address the problem more fully, e.g. discussion after class or a behaviour contract;

- devise follow-up strategies to deal with pupils after incidents, e.g. discussing with pupils their infringement of the rights of others, deciding on the consequences for their misbehaviour, deciding whether counselling is needed and putting pupils on behaviour contracts.

Key concept	★ Classroom discipline plan

■ The democratic approach

★ **R. Dreikurs**

Introduction

This approach is based on the idea that pupils have a basic **need for attachment** and social belonging. Pupils do not necessarily know how to achieve their goals of belonging to a group or class; sometimes they pursue **mistaken goals**. Teachers should strive to help pupils to achieve the goals of attachment and belonging. The best approach is to create a democratic classroom, to correct mistaken goals and to show pupils the right direction.

Theory

Democratic teaching is compared and contrasted with **autocratic** and **permissive teaching**. The democratic teacher helps pupils to develop self-discipline and self-motivation. The autocratic teacher dominates pupils and inflicts punitive consequences for rule-breaking. The permissive teacher allows a pupil to infringe rules with impunity and does not seek to foster a pupil's self-discipline. The democratic classroom is one where teachers and pupils collaborate in determining classroom rules and also the consequences for negative behaviour.

Dreikurs differentiates between praise and encouragement. Praise is where teachers inform pupils that they have performed a task well. Where pupils come to depend on praise they may fail to work to fulfil their own needs. Encouragement is where teachers recognise a pupil's efforts, help them to develop their strengths and lead them to feel that they are part of the class.

Pupils can pursue mistaken goals by seeking attention inappropriately from teachers and peers, by seeking power over teachers, by exacting revenge on teachers and by avoiding participation in classroom activities.

Practice

Self-discipline

Self-discipline is the ideal goal, to be contrasted with aversive discipline where unreasonable demands on pupils are backed up by harsh punishments; pupils react negatively against arbitrary discipline based on power assertion. Positive discipline enables pupils to experience freedom along with responsibility for the consequences of their behaviour. Consequences should be logical, not punitive.

Positive discipline is best achieved through collaboration between pupils and teachers. They should discuss and agree positive behaviours, classroom rules and the consequences for misbehaviour.

Autocratic teachers are characterised as coercive, demanding, dominating, hypercritical and punitive – the teacher's aim is to force pupils to behave and to deny them any freedom – while permissive teachers do not set limits nor do they establish logical consequences for misbehaviour. Democratic teachers are characterised as friendly, encouraging, collaborative, helpful, willing to share responsibility and stimulating.

Recognition

Pupils are seen as having a desire to belong to social groups and the class, as having free choice and at times as pursuing mistaken goals. These pupils are under the illusion that mistaken goals will enable them to gain positive recognition and status in the eyes of others. All pupils wish to achieve recognition and belonging. Some pupils hope to achieve recognition through misbehaviour because they think they cannot achieve it legitimately.

If pupils feel that they are denied recognition or that they do not belong, they will:

- attempt to gain the teacher's attention inappropriately by disrupting classroom routines, e.g. calling out, continually asking irrelevant questions, forever demanding the teacher's help, making loud noises, ceasing work and continually leaving their seat. Teachers who give in to this type of attention-seeking behaviour are likely to encourage or reinforce this form of misbehaviour;

- attempt to gain power over the teacher by, for example, arguing, refusing to comply with instructions, being verbally or physically aggressive and by lying. Pupils will feel empowered if they feel they have forced teachers into conflict situations;

- attempt to exact revenge on the teacher by misbehaving in a way that inevitably leads to punishment. Punishment is seen as justification for further acts of revenge;

- display inadequacy if these mistaken goals fail, i.e. avoiding or withdrawing from classroom activities. They appear apathetic, unresponsive and are passive and silent in their refusal to participate in classroom activities.

Redirection

Teachers are advised to **redirect** pupils so they can achieve recognition. This redirection can be realised through a series of steps:

- identifying the mistaken goal, i.e. seeking attention, acquiring power, seeking revenge or displaying inadequacy;

- pointing out to the pupil the mistaken goal and asking them what they hope to achieve through the pursuit of it;

- ignoring the behaviour if pupils are trying to gain inappropriate attention. When pupils are not demanding attention teachers should acknowledge them. If teachers are unable to ignore the attention-seeking behaviour they should respond in ways that do not reinforce it, e.g. by non-verbal communication or by private verbal communication;

- if pupils are trying to engage teachers in conflict, avoiding providing pupils with the opportunity to force them into conflict situations. Teachers can provide such pupils with legitimate means of aiming for power by giving them positions of responsibility or by enabling them to participate in decision making;

- if pupils are seeking revenge, providing opportunities that enable them to display their strengths;

- if pupils display inadequacy, being persistent in providing support and encouragement for any behaviour that shows progress no matter how insignificant. Teachers should also monitor their own reactions to pupils to prevent discouraging signals.

Encouragement

Teachers need to encourage their pupils if they are to increase their self-esteem. In order to encourage them teachers should:

- make positive and encouraging comments and avoid negative remarks;

- stress effort and improvement, not perfection;

- highlight strengths not weaknesses;

- emphasise that one can learn through making mistakes;

- develop pupil self-motivation and pupil self-satisfaction;

- create opportunities so pupils can experience success.

The use of encouragement can be counter-productive, for example if it invites competition and comparison, if it is lukewarm or if it is terminated if there is no response from the pupils.

Even where teachers consistently and persistently use encouragement pupil misbehaviour may occur. In these cases teachers should jointly agree with pupils **logical consequences** that will follow negative behaviours. Logical consequences should be differentiated from punishment: punishment is exacting revenge on pupils and encourages retaliation and the feeling that retaliation is justifiable. To be effective, logical consequences must be used consistently and should be related to the pupil's negative behaviour.

Pupil self-discipline is the ideal aim and can be developed through teachers:

- giving clear directions at an appropriate time;

- setting limits from the outset;

- establishing relationships based on trust and respect;

- making proportionate responses to negative behaviours;

- being fair as well as firm;

- showing respect for the pupil even when the pupil misbehaves;

- forgiving and forgetting past incidents, not bearing grudges.

Key concepts	★ Democratic teaching
	★ Autocratic teaching
	★ Permissive teaching
	★ Need for attachment
	★ Self-motivation
	★ Self-discipline
	★ Mistaken goals
	★ Logical consequences
	★ Redirection

Comment

Genuine joint decision making can help pupils to feel they are participants in classroom management. However, this can be very time-consuming and some pupils may never agree or agree publicly but disagree privately. Individual pupils may continue to disobey teachers and the class as a whole may also act defiantly. This largely preventative model does not address this eventuality.

■ The research-based empirical approach

★ **J. Kounin**

Introduction

Kounin's (1977) approach is based on research he undertook into the relationship between teaching methods and pupil behaviours. He researched in particular the relationship between teachers' desists (reprimands or comments) and pupil responses, and also the ripple effect of those desists on other pupils.

Theory

Generally it can be said that Kounin's approach is not based on any particular psychological or educational theory. It derives from research and is therefore an **empirical approach** not underpinned by any theoretical structure.

Kounin noticed a discrepancy between reports of pupils' classroom behaviours and observations of those same pupils in the classroom. As a consequence he emphasised the importance of classroom observation and also the videotaping of pupil behaviour.

He focused on teachers' responses to pupil behaviours and arrived at the conclusion that there was not a significant relationship between teachers' desists and older pupil behaviours. Instead he concluded that teachers should concentrate on using classroom management techniques that engage pupils in on-task behaviours.

Kounin lists a number of techniques that teachers can use to facilitate pupil on-task behaviour. These techniques are based on teachers being vigilant, i.e. being aware of how pupils are behaving in their classrooms and of their responses to pupils.

Practice

Techniques

- **Desists** are seen by Kounin as effective at nursery level if they are clear (naming the pupil, describing the specific misbehaviour, citing a reason for the desist) and firm. They do have a ripple effect on primary-aged pupils arising from both positive and negative comments on pupils' behaviours. Anger and mild punishment are not effective in changing behaviour. Desists do not have any significant effect on the behaviour of secondary-aged pupils. Where pupils like or respect teachers they behave better and work harder. Kounin's conclusion is that desists are not an effective technique for improving a particular pupil's behaviour or in discouraging other pupils from imitating that pupil's behaviour. However, desists are useful in the primary phase.

- **'Withitness'**, or teacher vigilance, is seen by Kounin as enabling teachers to be effective classroom managers. Teachers should be aware of how pupils are behaving in the classroom and also communicate that awareness to their pupils. Teachers must identify correctly pupils who are misbehaving, sort the behaviours into a hierarchy of severity and take prompt action before misbehaviour spreads or increases in severity.

- **Momentum and smoothness** also influence pupil behaviour. Momentum is where teachers commence activities on time. They should also effectively pace those activities and negotiate transitions and endings without disturbing the flow of lessons. Smoothness is where teachers avoid sudden changes in activities that unsettle pupils' thinking or working. The combination of momentum and smoothness are very effective in promoting positive pupil behaviour. Jerkiness, i.e. sudden changes in activities, disturb pupils who then engage in off-task and disruptive behaviours. Slowdowns are delays where teachers waste time by **overdwelling**, i.e. spend too much time on explanation, instruction, direction and correction of misbehaviours.

  For Kounin, momentum and smoothness are the two most important techniques for teachers to practise if they are to be effective classroom managers.

- **Group alerting** and **accountability** are ways in which teachers enable pupils to remain on task. Alerting is where teachers gain the attention of and impart instructions to pupils as quickly as possible. Teachers should aim to gain attention by asking questions that encourage all pupils to respond. Accountability is where teachers hold pupils responsible for what they are doing in the lesson. This involves teachers in monitoring pupils by asking them about their work.

- **Overlapping** is where teachers monitor or deal with two or more situations simultaneously, e.g. they can be engaged in assisting one pupil while correcting another.

- **Valence** is where pupils react positively or negatively to lessons. **Challenge arousal** is where teachers keep pupils alert by employing various techniques to revive pupil motivation or interest. Routine techniques are what teachers normally do to restore interest (e.g. pupils take turns), positive techniques are where teachers do something unusual to stimulate interest (e.g. throwing down a challenge) and negative techniques are where teachers superfluously repeat explanations and instructions. Kounin says that effective teachers use challenge arousal – i.e. they challenge their pupil – to revive pupil motivation. To be effective these challenges must be genuine, realistic and relevant. Teachers can also motivate their pupils through providing variety in terms of teaching style and presentation, e.g. the use of audio-visual methods and the restructuring of groups within the classroom. Finally teachers should ensure that pupils are aware that they are making progress in the subject area.

Key concepts	★ Empirical research ★ Desists ★ 'Withitness' ★ Momentum and smoothness ★ Overdwelling ★ Group alerting ★ Accountability ★ Overlapping ★ Valence and challenge arousal

Comment

Kounin's approach is based on his empirical observation of teachers in their classrooms. From this research he derives a series of correlations between teachers' classroom management techniques and pupil behaviour. These preventative techniques provide teachers with a means to reduce the probability of off-task or disruptive behaviour. Teachers certainly benefit from being vigilant in their classrooms through being aware of pupil interactions and by moving around the class in order to forestall problems. However, further measures are required in order to deal with disruptive pupils.

■ The behavioural approach

★ **I. Pavlov**

★ **B. Skinner**

Introduction

The behavioural perspective provides a simple, practical and effective approach, which can be a powerful agent of change in the classroom. Its principles are easy to learn, straightforward to apply and embody a systematic approach to assessment, formulation, intervention and evaluation of behavioural change. Some of its principles and methods are embedded within DfEE recommendations on the observation, recording and analysing of behaviour, for example applying functional analysis using the ABC.

Overview

This approach:

- emphasises current, overt, observable, behaviour;
- seeks to identify how the behaviour is reinforced and maintained;
- avoids predetermined labels to describe behaviour (e.g. medical, syndromes, etc.).

It is a theory of learning based on the assumptions that behaviour is:

- primarily a response to proximal (immediate), observable events;
- determined by its consequences;
- learnt, and therefore amenable to change or modification.

It is based on a scientific methodology such that:

- behaviour and its causes are assumed to be observable and measurable;
- behaviour can be clearly described;
- changes in behaviour, however small, can be systematically identified.

It provides a systematic methodology for behaviour assessment such that:

- pre-intervention baselines for later comparison are established;
- subjectivity is minimised;
- a testable hypothesis is formulated.

A systematic and objective approach is the hallmark of the behavioural perspective and is embedded within the DfEE document Circular 9/94 *The Education of Children with EBD*, which emphasises:

'... recording detailed observations to detect patterns of behaviour'.

In addition, the OFSTED Framework for the inspection of schools (May 1994) states that judgements should be:

'... secure: rooted in a substantial evidence base';

'... informed by ... quantitative indicators';

'... first hand ... based largely on direct observation of pupil's and teacher's work'.

The behavioural emphasis on direct observation of overt and thus, clearly describable and quantifiable behaviour leads to the 'substantial evidence base' required by OFSTED inspectors and of those teachers seeking to identify and evidence the 'strengths and weaknesses' of either:

- an institution;
- a group;
- an individual.

Theory: proponents, principles and concepts

I. P. Pavlov (1849–1936) – classical conditioning

In discovering that animal and human reactions were the consequences of conditioning, Pavlov had isolated a fundamental mechanism of learning. He adopted an empirical approach to the study of behaviour based on observation and measurement.

Classical or **respondent conditioning** describes the process of learning, applicable to desirable, deviant or maladaptive behaviour. It is concerned with the links between stimulus and response. It describes how a non-neutral or **conditioned stimulus** (i.e. food) produces an involuntary, automatic or unconditioned reflex response in an organism.

Conditioned stimulus		Unconditioned reflex response
food	=	salivation
light	=	constriction of pupils
heat	=	perspiration

A **neutral** or **unconditioned stimulus** (i.e. tone of voice, raised hand), paired with or contingent to a non-neutral stimulus, will become associated with non-neutral stimulus. Pavlov described this as a conditioned reflex, since the organism learns to respond (is conditioned) to the neutral, unconditioned stimulus in the absence of the original conditioned stimulus.

Contingency describes the relationship between behaviour, its antecedents (triggers) and its consequences (reinforcers).

```
┌─────────────────────────────────────────────────────────────┐
│              Pavlov's model of classical conditioning          │
│                    (stimulus–response theory)                  │
│                                                                │
│   conditioned stimulus              unconditioned response     │
│                                       (respondent behaviour)   │
│           food              =             salivation           │
│                                                                │
│                        unconditioned stimulus                  │
│         food      +    (a spoken word: 'dinner!') = salivation │
│                                                                │
│   unconditioned stimulus             conditioned response      │
│         response                      (respondent behaviour)   │
│         'dinner'            =             salivation           │
└─────────────────────────────────────────────────────────────┘
```

An example of classical or respondent conditioning: systematic desensitisation

By relaxing and at the same time imagining an anxiety-provoking object or situation in increasing proximity, the feared object is gently and gradually introduced. Symbolic objects such as photographs can be introduced; the real or imagined stimuli is then increasingly introduced, either through closer and closer physical proximity, or for increasing periods of time. By learning techniques to remain relaxed throughout these successive approximations a process of systematic desensitisation is achieved.

This technique can be used:

● with adolescents as part of anger management control programmes. Individuals or situations known to trigger an angry response are identified and then included in a programme of systematic desensitisation.

  • This would be coupled with additional cognitive-behavioural techniques focusing on self-monitoring and self-regulatory thinking.

  • It may also involve biofeedback procedures that identify attendant or ongoing physiological processes (breathing, heart-rate, etc.).

  Awareness of such processes enables monitoring of change and thus effects change, for example consciousness of hyperventilation may lead to slower, deeper breathing;

● with children making potentially difficult transitions.

  • Children beginning nursery education are gradually introduced.

  • Top juniors often visit their intended secondary school before term starts.

  • School-phobic pupils being reintegrated back into school after a prolonged period of non-attendance follow a partial timetable before being fully reintegrated.

A child has become fearful of PE and is allowed to increasingly take part in the sessions over a predetermined period of time. He or she:

- attends sessions to watch peers take part;
- changes into kit and watches peers take part;
- in kit, takes part in an identified/agreed part of the session;
- in kit, takes part in most of the session;
- in kit, takes part in the full session.

J. B. Watson (1878–1958)

Watson is famous for his experiments with 'Little Albert' (Watson and Raynor 1920). He identified a process whereby emotional responses are learnt.

Albert, an 11-year-old boy, became conditioned to fear rats after he began to associate their presence with a deliberately sudden, loud and frightening noise. Subsequent experiments showed that without further conditioning he had also become afraid of other furry animals – Watson called this 'generalisation'.

Key concepts	★ Conditioned stimulus/response
	★ Unconditioned stimulus/response
	★ Neutral stimulus
	★ Generalisation
	★ Discrimination
	★ Extinction

B. F. Skinner (1904–1990) – operant conditioning

Skinner took Thorndike's Law of Effect, developed it further and renamed it the **principle of reinforcement**. He identified everyday social reinforcers that shape behaviour and established that external contingencies were powerful factors in determining behaviour.

Contingency describes the relationship between a behaviour and the environmental conditions or events that proceed (**antecedent/** trigger) and follow (**consequence/**reinforce) the behaviour. **Operant conditioning** occurs where presentation of reinforcement is made dependent on or contingent upon an organism emitting a response. Any act – talking, revising for an exam and so on – that has an effect or operates on the environment and is reinforced may be described as operant behaviour.

The identification of contingencies is an important aspect of a behavioural assessment. Such contingencies are most usefully identified through observation. By understanding how antecedents and consequences influence behaviour, it is possible to formulate a hypothesis about what may change or modify behaviour.

Antecedents (A), Behaviour (B), Consequences (C) are the three components of a contingency		
A **Antecedent**	**B** **Behaviour**	**C** **Consequences**
• change of classroom	• noisy entrance to room	• teacher raises voice • noisy start to lesson
• when asked to sit and do written work	• child is out of seat frequently	• child gets attention from peers and teacher • child avoids written work

Positive reinforcement

If behaviour is observed to have increased in frequency, duration or intensity, it may be said to have been positively reinforced.

Common examples of positive reinforcement	
Positive reinforcer	**Positive reinforcement**
• high mark gained in test	• maintain or increase revision for next test
• teacher smiles and praises class when they enter room quietly	• class learns to enter classroom more quietly, more frequently

Positive reinforcement is a powerful shaper of behaviour:

• learning takes place when it is reinforced;

• reinforcers are, by definition, rewarding!

What is used as a reinforcer is significant. A teacher might consider a trip to a local burger joint to be exactly what the class would find rewarding for their improved behaviour. However, the class may not agree – given choices, they may vote for something quite different! It is important to ascertain what the individual or group themselves consider to be a rewarding event, token or experience – we are often surprised by choices which can be far less grand or sophisticated than we may expect.

Both behaviour and academic learning can be increased by reinforcing stimuli. Encouragement, praise and rewards are powerful shaping influences which contribute to motivation and positive learning patterns.

The Elton Report (DES 1989) emphasised the whole-school approach to behaviour which incorporates a 'balance' of rewards as well as sanctions. A whole-school approach encourages the involvement of the whole school community in establishing an ethos that is positive both academically and behaviourally. If positive elements supportive to the schools' stated ethos can be identified and reinforced, positive learning patterns, desired behaviours, high aspirations, pupils' efforts and so on are more likely to be maintained and/or increased.

- When a teacher is able regularly to mark the work of the class and return it when promised, there is an opportunity publicly and privately to reinforce the habit of completing and handing in class/homework.

- Favourable comments made publicly and/or privately communicate to the class not only the good results they have achieved individually, but the value the teacher places on such effort and attainment. Sharing such reinforcements publicly encourages motivation and promotes a shared and positive ethos. Even the tone of voice and smile of the teacher can be a reinforcer.

- Schools offering a range of rewards such as certificates, positive letters/phone calls home, a mention in assembly or the possibility of other treats and privileges, extend the number of potential reinforcers available to the teacher in the class. (However, it should be noted that some pupils find public praise very difficult. In such a case it may in fact be more punishing than rewarding, and thus become counter-productive. The teacher should try to become aware of and be sensitive to these individual needs.)

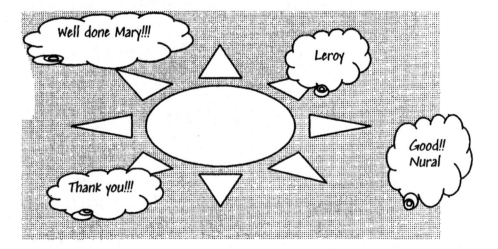

- Younger children often respond well to stickers or to charts that they can colour in. In *Perspectives on Behaviour* (Ayers, Clarke and Murray 1995) the authors describe how a class can be involved in working together on a few target behaviours which are monitored regularly on a large wall chart imaginatively designed to capture the children's interest and motivate them to support each other in achieving target behaviours.

Undesired behaviour can also be positively reinforced, often inadvertently. For example:

- a pupil calls out – the teacher responds – the calling out is reinforced;
- a pupil leaves their seat, avoids work and talks with friends – by doing so leaving the seat is reinforced;
- the class is noisy – the teacher keeps his or her voice raised – loud speaking is reinforced.

An ABC observation (p. 28) can help to identify unhelpful reinforcers.

Schedules of reinforcement

'Schedules of reinforcement' refers to the frequency and pattern of reinforcers. Most relevant to teachers are reinforcement schedules which are:

- constant, or
- intermittent.

- A teacher may decide initially to offer constant reinforcement to a class who are just beginning to learn to sit on the carpet and raise their hands when they wish to speak. The teacher may reinforce the whole group with descriptive praise – 'I'm so pleased to see how much effort you are all making to put up your hands' – while also rewarding individuals by responding to them when they have their hands up – 'Yes Syed, well done, you had your hand up, what would you like to say to us?'

- A target behaviour that has been initially well established may be subsequently reinforced by a reinforcer being presented at more intermittent and unpredictable intervals in relation to it. The interval and pattern of reinforcement can become less and less predictable.

- New behaviour is established more quickly with constant reinforcement.

- New behaviour is subsequently maintained with intermittent reinforcement.

- New behaviour becomes associated with reinforcers, and is maintained in the expectation or belief that reinforcement will be forthcoming.

Intermittent reinforcement is thus useful to maintain motivation, effort and established patterns of good behaviour.

Skinner described how the distribution and frequency of reinforcement affected the learning of new behaviour.

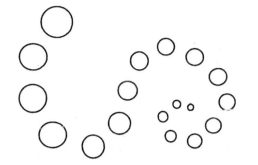

Each time the class responds to a non-verbal silent signal (a cardboard hand!) they will be awarded a sticker on the spiral.

A full spiral = a class party.

A spiral shape for stickers visually seems to show more frequent rewards at the onset of intervention, stickers appear to gather more slowly as the intervention progresses.

Extinction

Extinction occurs when behaviour is no longer reinforced.

Constantly reinforced behaviours may be susceptible to extinction. Behaviours established through intermittent reinforcers are less likely to become extinct when reinforcers are withdrawn.

- If a teacher **always** smiles and says 'Good morning' once the pupils have entered the classroom and sat down quietly, they are more likely to continue repeating their quiet entry into the room.

- If, however, the teacher **completely** stops smiling and greeting them, it will not be long before the pupils learn that their quiet entry into the classroom never elicits a favourable, rewarding response from the teacher – their entry into the classroom then deteriorates.

- If the teacher smiles, greeting the class **intermittently**, they will be more likely to continue to be motivated and maintain the desired behaviour.

An intermittent or thin reinforcer therefore reduces the possibility of the extinction of the behaviour, and is therefore a powerful mechanism in maintaining a favourable response – particularly when pupils may otherwise become bored with the chosen and perhaps limited range of reinforcers!

Extinction is seen to occur inadvertently when the young child constantly asks 'Why?' to her busy teacher. Her behaviour has previously been constantly and therefore effectively established at home by her parents. If in the busy classroom her questions pass unanswered, she quickly learns not to expect a satisfying response.

The principle of extinction is often used where:

- teachers deliberately ignore a particular behaviour – e.g. calling out – in order to avoid reinforcing it;

- teachers do not wish to draw attention to a particular behaviour – e.g. late arrival – and so avoid reinforcing that behaviour.

Instead of asking the class to be quiet, the teacher may hold up a hand for silence and then say 'Well done – that's how quietly I like to see you working', thus both describing clearly and reinforcing the desired behaviour, while ignoring and ultimately extinguishing the undesired behaviour.

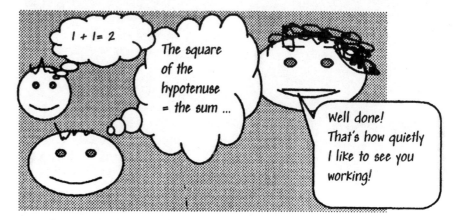

Negative reinforcement

If something has been taken away that the pupil does not like and the target behaviour is observed to have increased in frequency or intensity, it may be said to have been negatively reinforced.

Common examples of negative reinforcement	
Removal of aversive stimulus	**Negative reinforcement**
• will not have to resit exam	• maintain or increase revision for next test
• teacher will not write negative comment in the day book if pupils remember to enter the classroom quietly	• pupils enter classroom quietly
• detention removed if name rubbed off board for improved behaviour/effort	• improved effort/behaviour

It is often mistakenly thought that negative reinforcement is used to decrease a target behaviour. This is *not* the case!

Negative reinforcement should not be confused with punishment. Behaviour that is maintained or increased due to a stimuli/event which increases the likelihood of that behaviour occurring again cannot be said to be punishing, even though we might consider the stimuli to be 'negative' ourselves.

Negative reinforcement can have undesirable side effects:

• the teacher can become associated with the potential aversive event – thus damaging the relationship between pupils and teacher;

• pupils may try to escape or avoid the situation in which the possibility of an aversive stimuli is threatened – this has implications for internal and external truancy;

- if it is not used within the framework of techniques where positive reinforcement predominates, negative reinforcement may tend to be a less potent force for change and create a negative atmosphere in the classroom.

Punishment

Punishment occurs when a behaviour is observed to have decreased in frequency, duration or intensity: the behaviour may then be said to have been effectively punished.

Punishment is the presence of an aversive stimulus following on from and therefore associated with an undesired behaviour. At best it is a short-term strategy.

One form of punishment, 'response cost', describes the removal of a desired event, object or token. For example, points can be deducted, or playtime can be shortened.

Difficulties encountered with response cost are that pupils can begin to mistrust the points/tokens/reward system affected. Motivation may decrease and the relationship with the teacher deteriorates.

To avoid such difficulties it is best if response cost is not used where a system has been devised primarily as a reward. Once points, stickers and so on have been earned, they should not be taken away. Response cost operates most fairly in situations where points, tokens and so on are given initially to 'hold on to': misbehaviour is then followed by the loss of something given, rather than something earned.

To be effective, punishment should be:

- delivered immediately after the behaviour;

- delivered devoid of emotion;

- applied fairly and consistently.

Group or whole-class punishments should be avoided where possible.

Sanctions such as detentions, verbal reprimands or negative contact with the home, may be punishing in different degrees to different pupils. Sanctions should be:

- familiar to pupils before they are used;

- implemented after several warnings have been given;

- linked to the seriousness of the misbehaviour;

- consistently applied;

- used only where there also exists a balance of rewards.

Older pupils can be involved in devising a school Code of Conduct, while younger children can talk about and agree class rules.

The negative consequences of punishment are that:

- it does not educate pupils in what is expected of them (this is particularly true of younger pupils who need to hear explicit, descriptive statements about how the teacher wants them to behave);

- it risks alienating pupils and exacerbating already difficult behaviours;

- it can encourage 'devious' behaviour – the pupil tries harder not to be 'caught';
- it damages the relationship between pupil/class/teacher;
- it can promote withdrawn, depressed behaviour in certain pupils;
- it can create a negative class/school ethos;
- it can model aggressive, punitive style of relating to others;
- it can promote truancy;
- it has only a short-term effect on behaviour.

In addition:

- sanctions such as detentions, verbal reprimands, lines, poor reports, negative contact with the home may be punishing in different degrees to different pupils;
- a teacher who shouts at the pupils when their voices are raised and does not succeed in quietening the class is neither punishing nor managing their behaviour effectively.

Reprimands and other negative verbal statements expressing disapproval are generally considered to be unpredictable and achieve inconsistent results. Some of the simultaneous variables affecting the effectiveness are:

- tone of voice;
- method of delivery;
- accompaniment of additional aversive stimuli.

The accompaniment of additional aversive stimuli may help to ensure that punishment is more effective.

- Verbal reprimand is best backed up with action.
- For many pupils it is most effective to maintain eye contact during reprimand.

Some pupils feel challenged and may overreact to punishment. Difficult behaviour may escalate under what is experienced as a situation of impossible confrontation. As this is particularly disruptive to the classroom situation, teachers need to be aware of the pupils who are sensitive to this kind of interaction, or who perceive confrontation in otherwise apparently innocuous comments or actions.

What is considered by the teacher to be punishing may actually be experienced as rewarding by pupils. For punishment to be effective, we must know in advance what is considered or experienced as punishing by the pupils concerned. This may be ascertained by experience, i.e. the observation of a decrease in behaviour due to the presence of a stimuli perceived as negative by the class or individual.

There may also be sufficient number of reinforcers present in a situation to negate the punishment. For example:

- the desire for task avoidance is stronger than an aversion to detention;

- more satisfaction is gained from aggressive domination of peers than fear or discomfort is experienced from an adult reprimand and lack of peer friendship;

- greater delight and entertainment is experienced from joining peers in class disruption than fear or discomfort anticipated from later parental displeasure;

- the desire to lose temper and become aggressive is more satisfying than threat from fixed-term exclusion;

- depending on the pupil and the circumstances, an exclusion may itself be experienced as rewarding;

- as a more extreme example, the pleasures of group membership and peer approval outweigh the expense, initial anticipatory fears and subsequent addiction to heroin. The initial pleasurable mental and physical sensations of the drug also act as a reinforcer.

In this last example another mechanism of learning can be illustrated:

- negative reinforcement: taking the drug removes the immediate probability of an undesirable event – withdrawal symptoms.

Shaping

Shaping is said to occur when **successive approximations** to a desired behaviour are reinforced each time they occur. The desired behaviour is achieved by reinforcing each gradual step *en route*.

Shaping is often used by teachers with pupils who have either learning or behaviour difficulties. Encouragement and praise reinforce the responses which gradually approximate to the desired behaviour. For example, a child who is unable to write might first be reinforced when scribbling or 'drawing' on a piece of paper. As fine motor skills become more developed, the criterion will change by taking longer term targets into account.

Successive approximations in the first stages of learning to read may be defined, consistently reinforced and recorded thus:
- enjoys listening to stories;
- talks about stories read to him;
- refers to illustrations in retelling stories;
- makes simple predictions about stories;
- retells story without prompt.

For successful shaping to occur:

- pupils must be able partially to perform the desired behaviour already, therefore a clear assessment of their strengths and weaknesses is required;

- there are clear definitions of the desired behaviour;

- there are clear definitions of the success criteria;

- reinforcement is given consistently for target successive approximations.

As well as using positive reinforcers, it might also be necessary to use the extinction learning technique. For example, only reinforce those behaviours which have been targeted. Other extraneous or undesired behaviours should be ignored in accordance with the principles of extinction.

Target setting, when sensitively formulated, incorporates the concept of successive approximations. Early years and other teachers may associate the notion of successive approximations with 'Small Steps to Success' work. For example, an early years class are generally unsettled when gathered together to sit on the mat for afternoon registration. They are noisy, argumentative with each other, have a tendency to shout out to the teacher and often stand up and wander around the classroom. The teacher may decide upon the following targets:

- increase the length of time the class are seated on the mat;

- decrease the levels of noise when the class are seated on the mat;

- the pupils learn to sit with their hands in their laps when seated cross-legged on the mat;

- the pupils raise their hands if they want to speak to the teacher.

The teacher may prioritise the following targets:

. the pupils coming quietly to sit on the carpet;

2. the pupils sitting cross-legged on carpet with hands in their laps;

3. the pupils staying on carpet until requested to leave.

Successive approximations might include:

a) the pupils sit on mat at third request;

b) the pupils sit on mat at second request and cross legs when reminded;

c) the pupils sit on mat promptly at first request and cross legs without reminder.

Another example would be a small group of Year 6 pupils in the habit of wandering around the classroom, talking to peers, seeking teacher attention, and failing to organise their own equipment and complete sufficient work. They have developed a tendency repeatedly to ask for clarification and often leave their seats to talk to the teacher. The teacher may decide upon the following targets for this group:

- increase the time the group spends seated;
- develop their self-organisational skills;
- increase their volume of work;
- develop their presentation of work;
- increase their display of completed work.

The teacher may introduce the idea of individual task books which the pupils keep at their sides, and may prioritise the following targets:

1. each pupil independently reads a task written in the task book by the teacher;

2. the group agree and complete an equipment organisation checklist;

3. the group appoint one pupil to gather the necessary equipment;

4. the group check all the equipment collected by the appointed member;

5. the group remind each other to stay in their seats.

Successive approximations might include:

a) pupils write task in their task books which are checked by the teacher;

b) pupils write task in their task book and check it with another group member;

c) pupils raise their hands to show completed work to the teacher;

d) pupils read and check each other's work before showing it to the teacher;

e) pupils increase the number or complexity of tasks recorded in the book.

A further example is a class of EBD pupils attending a reintegration unit who complete very little work. The teacher decides to target:

- an increase in the production of completed work;
- development of collaborative working skills;
- development of an awareness of and ability to redraft;
- development of a sense of readership/audience for work;
- development of presentation skills.

The teacher decides to ask the group to produce a newspaper for distribution in schools. She may prioritise:

1. the completion of first drafts to be typed on to computer by the teacher;
2. the completion of second drafts to be typed on to the computer by the pupils;
3. the completed work to be proofread by other pupils before final typing.

Modelling describes the process whereby learning takes place through example. Modelling can incorporate successive approximations.

- A baby learns to speak through mimicking closer and closer approximations to the language of its significant others/primary carers.

- A child learns to take turns by taking part in small-group games where peers model the desired behaviour.

- A child observes learning or behaviour modelled by teachers and imitates that learning or behaviour.

Key concepts	★ Positive reinforcement
	★ Negative reinforcement
	★ Schedules of reinforcement
	★ Extinction
	★ Stimulus control
	★ Antecedents
	★ Consequences
	★ Prompting
	★ Fading
	★ Shaping
	★ Time out
	★ Response cost
	★ Contingency contracting
	★ Token economy

■ The cognitive and social learning approach

★ A. Beck

★ A. Ellis

★ A. Bandura

Introduction

This approach looks at how cognitions and **cognitive processes** influence the learning and behaviour of both teachers and pupils. Cognitions include beliefs and theories about learning and behaviour, self-image and self-esteem, attitudes and imaginings. Such cognitions may or may not be based on logical and empirical evidence.

The cognitive approach

Theory

The cognitive approach has been developed by A. Beck and A. Ellis, and is based on the idea of schemata, i.e. mental structures that process and interpret experiences. People can develop schemata that negatively interpret experiences, thus making them prone to emotional and behavioural problems or alternatively exacerbating them. People can also develop faulty or distorted ways of reasoning. Cognitions can be changed by questioning the empirical or logical foundations of thinking processes and belief systems.

Cognitive theory sees cognitions and changes in cognitions as affecting the way pupils learn and behave in the classroom. Pupils develop cognitions about the school and classroom context, about their teachers and about other pupils. In turn, teachers develop cognitions about the school and classroom context, about their pupils and about other teachers.

Faced by an external event teachers and pupils will process that event through internal mediation. They interpret or construct or give meaning to that event and relate that meaning to stored information and memories. New information is either assimilated into pre-existing **cognitive schemas** or cognitive schemas are accommodated to process new information. Therefore learning can be conceptualised as changes in cognitive schemas. Effective teaching facilitates changes in cognitive schemas.

Teachers may possess different and possibly conflicting theories or beliefs about the best way to teach and the ways in which pupils come to learn and behave, for example the use of phonics as against the 'real books' approach to reading, or the use of rewards as against the punishment approach to behaviour. Pupils may possess different levels of self-esteem or different notions of the roles of teachers.

These attitudes and beliefs, held rightly or wrongly, may influence classroom management for better or for worse.

Practice

Cognitive strategies are based on the idea that cognitive processes – in particular reasoning processes, attitudes and beliefs – need to be modified or changed if behaviour is to change.

Self-management is a **metacognitive** approach that encourages pupils to think about their own cognitive processes and how to modify or change them. The idea is to teach pupils how to monitor their environment with the aim of enabling them to identify the triggers that elicit learning and behaviour. Pupils are encouraged to set their own targets, record and evaluate their progress. By following this procedure they may be able to substitute more effective learning or behavioural responses. A progress chart or monitoring book can assist in this respect. Teachers are advised to implement verification procedures and to reinforce pupils for accurate recording and evaluation.

Self-reinforcement is an approach that encourages pupils to control and motivate themselves by rewarding or reinforcing their appropriate behaviour. Pupils are encouraged to set their own targets (self-prescription), monitor their own performance (self-monitoring), evaluate that performance (self-evaluation) and reward their own performance (self-reinforcement).

Self-instruction is an approach that derives from the ideas of Vygotsky (1962) who emphasised the importance of internal dialogues in enabling children to manage and control their behaviour. Behavioural problems are seen as arising from a lack of cognitive control either in terms of self-management or in terms of self-reinforcement. It is an approach that encourages pupils to instruct themselves in ways of reducing or eliminating the stress and anxiety that occurs in learning situations. Pupils are asked to reflect on their difficulties and to engage in an internal dialogue which might lead to more appropriate responses through the use of self-statements, i.e. the statements pupils make about themselves in difficult situations. First, this approach focuses on encouraging pupils to become aware of their difficulties and in particular on the negative self-statements they make about themselves. Pupils are then asked to substitute positive self-statements for negative ones. Finally pupils are encouraged to rehearse and then implement these positive self-statements in difficult situations.

Stress-inoculation training (Meichenbaum *et al.* 1985) is an approach that encourages pupils to learn how to cope with stress-evoking situations. Pupils are helped to produce positive coping statements in stressful situations. Anxiety- or stress-evoking situations are graded and pupils are asked to proceed through an anxiety hierarchy using positive coping statements, commencing with the least stressful situation. This procedure is often combined with training in relaxation techniques.

Problem-solving training (D'Zurilla and Goldfried 1971) is an approach that encourages pupils to proceed through a five-stage problem-solving model. The five stages are: 1) orientation or identification of the problem, 2) definition and formulation of the problem, 3) generation of alternative responses, 4) decision making and 5) verification of the problem solutions.

Reattribution (Bem 1972, Seligman *et al.* 1979, Weiner 1988) derives from Weiner's idea of achievement motivation, Seligman's notion of pessimistic style and Bem's theory of self-perception. It states that behaviours, feelings and attitudes often result from the way people make causal attributions about situations or events. Certain kinds of causal attributions can result in negative learning and behaviour. Pupils are perceived as having particular kinds of **attributional styles** which have positive or negative consequences for them. They can also be seen as having an internal or external **locus of control** (Rotter 1971). Internals see themselves as being able to change their behaviour whereas externals see their behaviour as being produced and controlled by others. This approach encourages pupils to modify or change the causal attributions they make about their difficulties, particularly in terms of success and failure. Pupils are taught to substitute positive causal attributions for negative ones. Another method is to change the problem situation in a way that elicits positive attributions instead of negative ones.

Cognitive restructuring includes Beck's (1970) cognitive approach and Ellis's (1977, 1979) rational-emotive approach. This concerns itself with belief systems that are seen as influencing behaviour across a range of contexts. Pupils are seen as holding faulty or irrational beliefs that adversely affect their behaviour. The aim of cognitive restructuring is to modify or change these beliefs in a way that leads to a change in behaviour. Pupils are seen as having accumulated through their past experiences negative beliefs about themselves and others, these beliefs resulting from, for example, unwarranted generalisations from particular instances. Teachers need to identify their pupils' faulty thinking or irrational beliefs and present and discuss alternative ideas and beliefs.

Key concepts	★ Cognitive processes
	★ Cognitive schemas
	★ Metacognition
	★ Self-control
	★ Self-reinforcement
	★ Self-instruction
	★ Stress-inoculation
	★ Problem-solving
	★ Attributional style
	★ Locus of control
	★ Cognitive restructuring
	★ Cognitive distortions
	★ Rational and irrational beliefs
	★ Reattribution

The social learning approach

Theory

The social learning approach has been developed by A. Bandura. According to this theory there is an interaction between people and their environment, which is known as 'reciprocal determinism'. People influence their environment and their environment influences them. People's self-conceptions and self-regulation are seen as varying according to their situation or circumstances. A fundamental concept is that of self-efficacy or the perceived ability of a person to perform effectively a given task or in a given situation. People's **self-efficacy** will influence their learning and behaviour.

This theory sees learning as arising from pupils observing and imitating or modelling themselves on others.

Observational learning occurs when people learn by observing the behaviour of others. This way they can learn or acquire new behaviours independent of these behaviours being reinforced.

Vicarious reinforcement occurs when pupils observe (**acquire**) the behaviour of teachers and other pupils and model or imitate (**perform**) those behaviours. If during the observation or acquisition phase pupils see the behaviour reinforced then they will probably acquire the behaviour. However, if the behaviour is punished then they will probably not acquire it. This form of reinforcement provides information and helps to motivate pupils. Continued operant reinforcement of pupils' behaviours will often be necessary for them to maintain the appropriate behaviours.

Effective **modelling** requires models to meet certain preconditions, i.e.

- they must be seen to possess competence and status;

- they must present realistic yet achievable performances;

- they must appear as caring.

Self-regulation occurs when peoples' behaviours are seen as being influenced and maintained by expectancies or anticipated consequences. People also reward themselves, a process of self-reinforcement, if they reach a given standard. This in turn serves to motivate them. Behaviour is seen as also being influenced by peoples' own cognitive processes.

Practice

Teachers model behaviours all the time and they should be aware of the positive and negative effects of their modelling on their pupils. Modelling techniques include:

- using video representations of model behaviours;

- using peers as models to demonstrate new behaviours;

- using peers to tutor other pupils in new behaviours;

- implementing a 'buddy' system where a role model is paired with a problem pupil to assist that pupil in learning new behaviours;

- when a problem pupil is misbehaving in a specific way, focusing attention on a pupil who is behaving in an opposite and positive way.

Key concepts	★ Reciprocal determinism ★ Self-efficacy and expectancies ★ Observational learning ★ Vicarious reinforcement ★ Acquisition ★ Performance ★ Self-regulation ★ Modelling ★ Guided participation

■ The assertive discipline approach

★ **L. Canter**

Introduction

This approach is based on the idea that pupils and teachers have rights as well as responsibilities. Pupils need and respond to limits set by teachers and teachers therefore should ensure those limits are established. In order to establish limits teachers need active support from school management and from parents. Teachers also need to instruct pupils in positive behaviour and discuss with disruptive pupils the problems they present in the classroom.

Theory

A positive classroom atmosphere is established through meeting pupils' needs, planning and implementing effective classroom rules, teaching pupils how to behave appropriately, providing positive attention and engaging in productive dialogue with disruptive pupils. Teachers are described as **assertive** if they effectively communicate the behaviour required of their pupils and the actions by which they intend to achieve this behaviour. Appropriate positive actions must follow words otherwise responses are non-assertive and therefore ineffective.

Teachers must respond positively to pupils who display appropriate classroom behaviour, thus recognising their efforts to achieve the teacher's goals. It is important that teachers are sincere when recognising pupils' attempts to meet their expectations.

Where pupils fail to meet teachers' expectations, they must learn that certain negative consequences will ensue, but these consequences should not physically or psychologically damage pupils.

Practice

This approach to classroom management is based on the idea of developing and implementing a '**classroom discipline plan**'. This plan includes **rules**, **positive recognition** and **consequences**. The aim of this approach is also to teach pupils responsible behaviour and to develop individualised behaviour plans.

The classroom discipline plan
Aims
- To achieve a safe classroom environment.
- To enable teachers to teach effectively.
- To facilitate pupils' learning.

Benefits
- It avoids *ad hoc* and inconsistent responses towards pupils.

- It encourages fairness in dealing with pupils.
- It helps to reduce disruptive behaviour and thereby enables all pupils to learn.
- It elicits parental support.
- It communicates to school management and inspectors that there is a planned approach to classroom behaviour management.

Developing the classroom plan

General rules

These rules are appropriate for all contexts and classroom activities. They should be clear and unambiguous and also be observable, i.e. a teacher or pupil can see an example of the rule being followed or met. There should not be too many rules and they should be appropriate for the teacher, context and activity. The rules should be realistic and enforceable. Pupils should also be involved in choosing the rules.

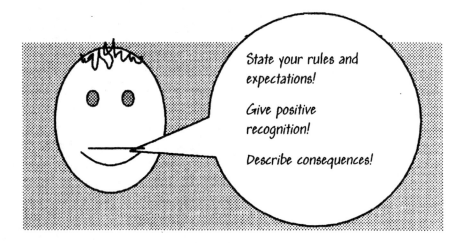

Positive recognition

The aim is to positively recognise the efforts of pupils to meet teachers' expectations. Pupils will feel encouraged if their efforts are accorded recognition and this will help raise their self-esteem and improve their behaviour. Positive recognition should also be given to the whole class where appropriate, i.e. where there is a specific classroom problem. It can be communicated to pupils through praise, contact with home, awarding privileges, certificates and material rewards.

Praise, to be effective, should be personal, sincere, specific and descriptive. Pupils will appreciate praise that recognises them as an individual, that is sincerely expressed and that specifically relates to a positive behaviour they have performed. The manner and way in which this praise is communicated to pupils is very important and should take into consideration the sensitivities of the pupils concerned.

Contact with home has positive benefits for teachers. Parents will appreciate positive communication from teachers as they are often only contacted if there are problems at school. Parents can feel pride in their children and contribute to positive behaviour by adding their praise, reinforcing that of the teachers. A positive home–school relationship can thereby be facilitated and developed, which will pay dividends in the future.

Privileges and certificates given to pupils often have a positive motivating effect even with those who appear indifferent or who are in the higher age groups. Pupils can, for example, be awarded with special passes or positive commendations.

Material rewards can be given to those pupils who do not respond to praise, privileges or commendations. Rewards should be given soon after the pupil performs the positive behaviour and should be accompanied with descriptive praise from the teacher.

Consequences

Teachers should plan consequences for when pupils do not observe classroom rules. Consequences should be presented as choices which pupils make when they disobey class rules. The consequences should be proportionate to the offence and they must be experienced as unwelcome by pupils but not as physically or psychologically damaging. Consequences should be arranged in a hierarchy which teachers ascend depending on the seriousness of the offence. It helps to have a sheet to record pupils' behaviours in terms of day and time and the consequences of pupil behaviours.

Some suggested consequences are keeping pupils in for a short time after class, separating pupils from each other and requiring pupils to write an account of their behaviour for teachers and parents.

Implementing the plan

Plans should be discussed with headteachers so that they know that before pupils are sent to them teachers have implemented discipline plans. These plans should be discussed with pupils, rules should be explained and pupils' understanding of these rules should be established. Consequences of infringements of the rules should also be explained. A copy of the plan should be sent to parents.

Teaching responsible behaviour

Directions should be specified for all classroom activities in order that pupils know teachers' expectations. Pupils must be motivated to follow these directions: this motivation can be facilitated through positive recognition. Various techniques can be used to communicate positive recognition:

- Positive repetition requires the teacher to give a direction, identify those pupils following the direction and then recognise this by verbally restating the direction as pupils perform it.

- Consistent praise is where teachers are continually on the lookout for opportunities to praise pupils. This praise should be personal, specific and descriptive.

- Scanning requires teachers to look up every few minutes when working with an individual pupil or small group. By being vigilant teachers will notice pupils who are on task and be able to recognise their positive behaviour. Teachers will also see pupils who are off task and make those pupils aware that they have been spotted and encourage them to get back on task.

- Circulating the classroom requires teachers to move around the classroom complimenting pupils for being on task and for the quantity and quality of their work.

Where pupils are engaging in off-task behaviour that does not disrupt other pupils then the advice is to provide an opportunity for pupils to become on task without using loud reprimands. Instead, the use of a questioning 'look' or just physically being near the pupils may be sufficient to prompt pupils to become on task. Alternatively it may be effective just to mention the pupil's name or to praise pupils nearby who are on task.

Consequences should be implemented consistently in a calm but firm manner. Teachers should be on the lookout for opportunities to praise pupils for positive behaviour who have been sanctioned in the past for misbehaving. Where pupils question consequences teachers should defuse potential conflict by offering pupils the opportunity to write down their account of an incident or arrange to discuss the incident after the lesson is over.

With some pupils who persist in misbehaving it may be helpful to remind pupils of consequences they have experienced in the past and consequences that might be implemented in the future if there is further misbehaviour.

With the small minority of difficult pupils further advice is as follows:

- Hold problem-solving conferences where teachers discuss specific behaviour difficulties with pupils. These provide an opportunity for pupils to express their thoughts and feelings, enable teachers to discover what is causing the problem and allow time to discuss with pupils ways in which they could choose to rectify problems.

- Develop positive support for pupils through teachers showing an interest in pupils' leisure activities, disclosing some personal but not intimate facts that engage pupils' interests and sending complimentary notes to pupils. Other ways are greeting pupils when they come into the classroom, providing personal attention in the form of asking pupils how they are or how they are getting on, and visiting or phoning pupils' homes as a means of conveying positive messages.

- Develop individualised behaviour plans analogous to classroom behaviour plans. This type of plan should specify two or three significant target behaviours, a hierarchy of consequences for misbehaviour, positive recognition for appropriate behaviours and ways of achieving parental involvement and contact.

- Facilitate support from parents and senior management through teachers providing information on measures taken to deal with problem behaviours. Teachers should record actions taken to solve the problems.

Key concepts	★ Pupils' and teachers' rights and responsibilities ★ Assertive teaching ★ Classroom discipline plan ★ Rules, positive recognition, consequences

Comment

This approach appears at least in part to be based on an operant model, for example positive recognition can be understood as a form of positive reinforcement. Consequently this approach shares the advantages and disadvantages of any model based on behaviourism. There has also been debate over whether extrinsic motivation, encouraged by the model, prevents or undermines the development of intrinsic motivation. Furthermore this approach appears to cast pupils in purely passive roles as recipients of teachers' interventions.

Teachers should be sensitive to individual differences among their pupils, for example some pupils respond to positive recognition while others do not; some respond to consequences while others do not.

Sometimes the ways in which positive recognition and consequences are used are counter-productive. Pupils may not like positive recognition made public. They may not like teachers inquiring into their personal lives or contacting parents. There should be a degree of flexibility in developing discipline plans because too rigid an approach will not encompass changing circumstances.

This model, like others, is dependent on a whole-school behaviour policy, where teachers agree on a common and consistent approach to behaviour problems across the school.

■ The ecological and ecosystemic approaches

★ **A. Molnar**

★ **B. Lindquist**

Introduction

These approaches are based on the idea that problems in classroom management arise out of negative systemic interactions or a negative environment. This means that classroom problems can be seen as being a function of interactions between different conflicting systems or people in conflict within and between those systems. It also means that the physical environment itself can positively or negatively affect the classroom. By intervening systemically or by changing the environment, positive or negative effects can be effected.

Theory

The ecosystemic approach

This is based on Systems Theory, which sees a system – for example a school or a classroom – as being composed of subsystems that interconnect and influence each other to varying degrees. Such a system can be influenced by external systems and can influence external systems. Changes in a system or subsystem can affect other systems and subsystems. The mutual influence of systems and subsystems is a form of recursive causality. Classroom management problems are seen as a product of negative interactions between teachers and pupils and between pupils themselves.

The ecological approach

This regards the physical environment as having an influence on classroom management. This approach states that certain factors – such as amount of space, use of space, personal space, seating arrangements, temperature, noise and class size – need to be considered in terms of their implications for classroom management. This approach also considers the impact of parents and families on schools and ultimately on classroom management.

Practice

The ecosystemic approach

Ecosystemic techniques concentrate on examining the implications teacher–pupil interactions have for classroom management. Teachers are asked to reflect on their attitudes and expectations of their pupils and find out how they may be contributing to problems in their classrooms. Teachers should examine their perceptions of a particular class or form and see how they affect it. If teachers decide that their perceptions are negative and are contributing to problems that they have with the class or form then they are urged to employ the technique of **reframing**: they interpret all the behaviour of a class as having positive effects – for example misbehaviour of pupils in a bottom stream can be interpreted as a reaction to what they perceive as negative labelling and as a result a wish for positive recognition from teachers. On reframing the misbehaviour teachers can then think of ways of giving the class positive recognition that will have a positive impact on their behaviour.

The ecological approach

Ecological approaches look at aspects of the classroom environment and their implications for classroom management.

- **Seating arrangements**. Teachers should consider how the seating arrangements in their classrooms affect learning and behaviour. Pupils may, if left to choose their classroom locations, choose positions which detract from learning. Pupils who are high in self-motivation may choose seats near the teacher; others, who are disaffected, may sit at the back. Participation levels may be enhanced for those in front seats and decreased for those in the rear seats. The idea that seating positions may affect levels of pupil participation, attention and achievement is known as the environmental hypothesis. Where pupils choose their own seating arrangements this may create or exacerbate class misbehaviour. Disaffected pupils may sit together and reinforce each other's misbehaviour, forming a counter-culture within the class. This in turn may have a ripple effect on other borderline disaffected pupils. It is advisable to seat pupils where possible to a plan that encourages an optimal mix of learning and behaviour. Where pupils have established a chosen place or choice of seat this often becomes their personal space which, if invaded, then makes negative interactions likely. Teachers should be aware that pupils develop notions of place ownership and use and that these notions can have positive and negative implications for classroom management. In mixed-sex classes teachers should also be aware of their pupils' perceptions of being asked or required to sit next to pupils of a different gender.

- **External conditions**, e.g. time of day, noise and temperature. Pupils' learning performance generally increases as the day progresses. This should be borne in mind when setting extremely complicated tasks. With regard to noise, pupils may not hear teachers clearly as the noise level rises or pupils may become distracted and pay more attention to those sitting nearby than to the teachers. Teachers may end up shouting to be heard, which becomes wearing for them and can lead to pupils developing negative perceptions of them. With regard to temperature, an overheated or an underheated classroom may lead to a deterioration in learning and behaviour. Pupils will focus on their discomfort and teachers will spend a considerable proportion of the lesson on fielding complaints about the heat or the cold.

- **Class size**. There appears to be controversy over the effects of class size on learning. A positive effect of small class size has been identified during the first years of schooling and on socially disadvantaged pupils, particularly those from ethnic minorities. It has been pointed out that one needs to consider class size and teaching methods together. It is difficult, if not impossible, for teachers to effect a reduction in class size but where a reduction occurs teachers should consider whether a change in teaching methods is mandated.

- **Teacher expectations**. Teachers' beliefs about their pupils can affect their pupils learning and behaviour, sometimes known as the expectancy or Pygmalion effect (Rosenthal and Jacobsen 1968). Teachers should reflect on the expectations they have of their pupils, considering whether they are too high, too low or not high enough. Where teachers label pupils as 'thick' or 'bad' this may result in those pupils becoming disaffected or becoming more disaffected. Labelling can amplify deviance. With regard to gender, different expectations teachers may have of boys and girls may affect learning and behaviour. Similarly, with respect to ethnicity teachers may develop negative stereotypes of certain ethnic groups which then affect learning and behaviour. Teachers should reflect on their concepts and images of gender and ethnic differences and their implications for classroom management. Pupils expect teachers to be responsive to their personal needs, i.e. they expect teachers to see them as persons in their own right, not as having a particular gender or belonging to a particular ethnic group.

Classroom environment research

This research (e.g. Moos 1979) has contributed towards evaluating the interaction between pupils and their environments. Moos terms his model 'social-ecological', which means that interactions between personal and environmental systems have to be considered. He identifies four elements of the environment: the physical setting, organisational aspects, intake factors and ethos. The personal system is seen as composed of the pupil's expectations, values and coping strategies. These two systems interact but are mediated through selection, cognitive appraisal, motivation, adaptation and coping.

School effectiveness research

This research (e.g. Rutter *et al.* 1979, Mortimore *et al.* 1988) has arrived at the conclusion that there is a school effect whereby, even allowing for intake differences, schools can differ in their effectiveness in terms of learning and academic outcomes. Research recommendations have emphasised the importance of a structured learning environment. A structured environment is one where teachers strive to develop and implement a consistent approach to teaching and learning, encouraging their pupils to become active participants in the learning process. Teachers are also encouraged to develop and use a balanced and flexible combination of individual, group and class teaching.

Teachers are urged by Reynolds (1985) to implement what he describes as an incorporative strategy and avoid using a coercive strategy with their classes. An incorporative strategy is one where teachers enable pupils to acquire a sense of responsibility for their learning and behaviour and to feel that they share with teachers control over the learning process. A coercive strategy is one where teachers use coercive methods such as an overreliance on punishment to manage their classes.

Teachers are encouraged by Hargreaves, Hestor and Mellor (1975) to develop what is termed a 'deviance-insulative' strategy and avoid a 'deviance-amplification' strategy. A deviance-insulative strategy is one that, for example, avoids confrontations and unfairness, shows respect for pupils and manages the class sympathetically and with humour. A deviance-provocative or amplification strategy sees conflict with pupils as inevitable, resulting in the teacher managing the class through confrontation, threats and inconsistent punishment.

Badger (1985) in his research points out that disruptive behaviour is not simply random within a school but can be influenced by factors such as the ratio of boys to girls (2.75:1), the day of the week (Monday), the period of the day (last period in the afternoon), particular pupils (five pupils accounting for 11 per cent of referrals to quiet room), particular teachers (five staff accounting for 30 per cent of referrals to quiet room) and the approach of half-terms. He concluded that various school-based factors influenced disruptive behaviour, such as particular recidivist pupils who were often low achievers, a small number of pupils presenting severe behavioural problems who the school could not control, teachers who were perceived by pupils as 'loud', 'too soft', 'not listening', 'not doing anything about ...', 'late' and 'inconsistent', spillover effects on lessons from the behaviour of classes in previous lessons and pupils resistant to theoretical as against practical subject content. Badger also states that whole-school factors influenced disruptive behaviour, for example teachers not having classroom bases, chaotic movement between lessons, inadequate or an absence of a code of conduct, failure to enforce rules or inconsistent enforcement of school rules, inadequate communication between staff as perceived by pupils, teachers feeling isolated in their classrooms and teachers having insufficient time for their pupils.

These suggestions depend on schools developing and implementing effective whole-school policies. The aim of these policies is to bring about consistent yet flexible approaches to learning and behaviour in schools and in particular in classrooms. Generally speaking pupils respond positively to consistency and will react negatively to inconsistency. Furthermore pupils will respond positively to high expectations of their work and behaviour, to positive modelling by teachers and positive feedback from teachers. Whole-school policies must be clear, realistic, achievable and relate to the school's particular context.

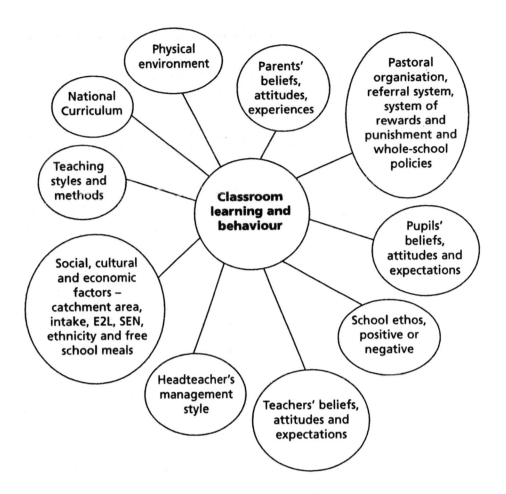

Ecological influences on classroom learning and behaviour

Key concepts	**Ecosystemic approach** ★ Systems and subsystems ★ Cycles of interaction ★ Positive and negative interactions ★ Reframing **Ecological approach** ★ Recursive causality ★ Physical, social and cultural context ★ School ethos ★ Seating and grouping ★ Streaming, setting and mixed ability ★ Expectations ★ Class size

Chapter 4

Special categories of pupils

■ Pupils with conduct disorder (severe behavioural difficulties)

Introduction

These pupils are described as experiencing severely disrupted relationships with parents, teachers and peers and as having a low level of educational attainment or as underachieving. They are often referred to a wide range of agencies, for example the police, social services, the educational social work service (ESWS), the educational psychology service (EPS) and child guidance.

Definition

This kind of pupil shows a persistent pattern of negative behaviour that disrupts his or her education and that of his or her peers. The pupil will manifest some or many of the following behaviours: stealing, running away from home, lying, arson, truancy, theft, vandalism, cruelty to animals or people, sexual harassment, carrying or use of a weapon and frequent fighting. The frequency, duration and severity of the pupil's misbehaviour have to be considered. Delinquency occurs where pupils break the law and are charged with an offence. The earlier the onset of problems the greater the probability the child will maintain criminal behaviour into adulthood.

Some of these pupils display hyperactivity or ADHD (attention deficit/hyperactivity disorder), experience low levels of academic achievement, drop out of school or leave school without qualifications. Some may have poor interpersonal and problem-solving skills resulting in them being rejected by their peers or in having negative interactions with adults. Some also experience anxiety and depression.

They may have parents with psychiatric disorders, criminal records or who are alcoholics. Some of these parents often use punitive and coercive discipline and can be child abusers. Parental discipline is frequently inconsistent, oscillating between harshness and laxity. Supervision is often poor. Family or parental discord is often present.

They may associate with and imitate a delinquent peer group. In cognitive terms they may be hypersensitive to what they misconstrue as hostile behaviour, for example people looking at them or knocking into them.

Interventions

Pupils who are assessed as having severe behavioural difficulties or conduct disorders can be helped or managed through using a variety of interventions.

Cognitive-behavioural techniques

Teachers can use some of these techniques in the classroom with such pupils. Behavioural techniques can be effective if applied consistently and used persistently. It is important to note that teachers can positively reinforce bad as well as good behaviour. Sending pupils out of the class may be experienced as rewarding for a pupil who would prefer to avoid work or who would like to join others sent out of classes.

- **Positive reinforcement** or the rewarding of good behaviour: in order to be effective, positive reinforcement must be frequent, consistent, persistent and contingent upon appropriate behaviour. Rewards must motivate the pupil.

- **Punishment** should take the form of withdrawal of reinforcers, e.g. time out from reinforcement or response cost (see p. 33), the loss of a positive reinforcer.

- **Contingency contracting** is where the teacher in consultation with the pupil and parents comes to a joint decision in the form of either an informal verbal agreement or in formal printed documents. They must be made contingent on appropriate behaviour. The contract usually specifies SMART targets, success criteria, rewards, sanctions and a method of evaluation. Contracts can serve as a means of linking school and home.

- **Changing antecedents and/or consequences**. Behavioural change can be facilitated through applying an ABC analysis (see p. 28) to a disruptive pupil's behaviour. This analysis can identify the events leading to a pupil's aggression and the reinforcing events that follow a pupil's aggression. An ABC analysis enables teachers to change the antecedents, e.g. seating arrangements, group or form, or change the consequences, e.g. removing the pupil from reinforcers in the classroom.

- **Social skills training** focuses on the training of pupils in verbal and non-verbal communication skills that lead to improved social interactions with adults and peers. Pupils must have an actual social skills deficit and not simply be unwilling to use their social skills in particular settings. In the classroom teachers can model the kinds of behaviour they would like the pupil to imitate and avoid displaying negative behaviours themselves.

- **Problem-solving skills training** focuses on a pupil's cognitive processes, particularly problem-solving skills, self-statements, attributions and perceptions, which are seen as contributing to behaviour problems. A pupil's verbal and physical aggression is regarded as being due to the ways the pupil misconstrues the behaviour of teachers and other pupils. In particular such pupils tend to be hypersensitive to what they regard as hostile looks. This approach attempts to get pupils to make positive reattributions, e.g. by construing what they normally regard as hostile actions as neutral. Pupils are also asked to substitute positive for negative self-statements. In addition they can be encouraged to adopt a problem-solving approach whereby they generate alternative solutions to their difficulties.

- **Parent management training** focuses on the parent's approach to discipline. Parents are encouraged to reinforce good behaviour, to ignore minor misbehaviour and to avoid positively reinforcing negative behaviour. They are also asked to avoid using physical punishment and instead to use time out and the withdrawal of privileges. Interventions with parents should be linked where possible to similar interventions in the classroom.

- **Self-monitoring** can be an aid to helping pupils become aware of the triggers that elicit their behaviour. A variety of self-monitoring methods can be used depending on the pupil's level of cognitive, personal and social development, e.g. by using a graph, chart, diary or stop-watch. It is advisable that self-monitoring is used from the beginning, i.e. when the pupil first begins to misbehave. Pupils can be taught to identify internal and external cues that trigger their misbehaviour and this can be a step on the way to those pupils controlling their behaviour.

- **Modelling** is where a teacher demonstrates the desired behaviour or shows ways of resolving conflicts *in vivo* or through role-play. The teacher can then ask the pupil to rehearse the behaviour that has been modelled by the teacher.

Comment

With pupils displaying severe behavioural difficulties it is advisable for teachers to avoid heavy confrontations or power struggles in the classroom. Sometimes it is possible for teachers to detect that the pupil has come to school in a bad mood and head off a possible confrontation. Teachers should be consistent, calm, firm and fair in implementing correction and, if possible, this should take place in private outside the classroom or at the end of a lesson. Pupils can be quick to detect discrepancies in the ways other pupils are treated. It should be made apparent to pupils that they are respected as persons but that their misbehaviour is unacceptable. Where it is possible pupils should be given opportunities to exercise responsibility. Teachers should also avoid sarcasm or making derogatory remarks about the pupil's dress, appearance or background. It can be the case that pupils who misbehave with one teacher may not misbehave with others. Reasons for this should be established. A change of form, class or teacher may have a positive effect on all concerned. Continual punishment may prove ineffective and it is often desirable to use a balanced combination of rewards and sanctions. Harsh punishments may prove counter-productive.

Key points	★ Often negative relationships with parents, teachers and peers ★ Frequency, duration and severity of misbehaviour ★ Disrupts own and others' education ★ Can be associated with learning difficulties, ADHD, delinquency **Symptoms** ★ Physical aggression, lying, carrying or using a weapon, cruelty ★ Vandalism, arson, theft ★ Truancy, school failure, running away from home ★ Substance misuse **Risk factors** ★ Parents with criminal records or who are abusers, family conflict ★ Inadequate parenting – inconsistent disciplining, lack of supervision ★ Poor social, interpersonal, problem-solving and learning skills ★ Association with a delinquent peer group

■ Pupils with attention deficit/ hyperactivity disorder

Introduction

These pupils are described as experiencing severe problems in paying and maintaining attention (ADD) and in some cases as also being overactive (ADHD). The diagnosis is made by a psychiatrist or physician using DSM IV or ICD 10.

Definition

The pupil who experiences ADHD displays inattentiveness, impulsivity and overactivity. There may be associated difficulties such as underachievement, truancy, learning difficulties, aggressiveness, substance misuse and peer rejection. In order for there to be a diagnosis of ADHD the symptoms must occur in two settings – for example home and school – and occur with different task demands. The symptoms must also have occurred before the age of seven years, have existed for six months and be developmentally inappropriate. There is some overlap with conduct disorder: estimates vary between 30 per cent and 90 per cent. Estimates of the prevalence depend on definitions but the consensus is between 3 per cent and 5 per cent. There is believed to be a genetic predisposition to ADHD and there is also a suggestion that frontal lobe malfunctioning is associated with it. The child who has ADHD can make parenting a very stressful experience.

Interventions

There are a number of different approaches to dealing with pupils who have ADHD. Generally when teaching a pupil who has ADHD it is wise to use a structured, consistent and graduated approach which enables the child to experience a predictable routine. Where possible teachers should establish and maintain conditions that enable the pupil to avoid being distracted. This means placing him or her in an appropriate place in the classroom. Instructions should be clear and concise. Work should be varied and broken down into short steps. The teacher should concentrate on getting the pupil on task and completing work, thus avoiding the use of constant reprimands for misbehaviour. Feedback should be frequent.

- **Psychostimulant medication**, usually Ritalin or methylphenidate, is prescribed for children with ADHD by a psychiatrist or physician. This drug has a positive but short-term effect on between 70 per cent and 80 per cent of children; it is used to manage the problem and is not a cure. The average time on the drug is from two to seven years. It is given in the form of short- and long-term acting tablets, and increases the level of arousal in the brain. There can be negative side effects, e.g. sleeping problems and weight loss, and 20 per cent to 30 per cent of children do not respond to Ritalin. The use of medication is based on the theory that the effects of ADHD are the result of neurotransmitter malfunctions in the frontal lobe of the brain which lead to the child being in a state of continuous underarousal. The drug is thought to stimulate the parts of the brain that increases arousal and attention but it does not permanently affect brain chemistry.

- **The behavioural approach** uses a programme of positive reinforcement and punishment. Pupils should be rewarded for paying attention, staying in their seats and completing work. Rewards should be given immediately after the performance of the positive behaviour, and where possible should take the form of the pupil choosing a preferred activity. Where pupils are disobedient they should be given time out, and this can also be used where a pupil experiences positive reinforcement for misbehaviour, e.g. inappropriate attention from peers or even the teacher: the pupil is given time out from the classroom. This intervention should be of short duration. Reprimands should be given quietly and calmly. Another technique is 'ignore-rule-praise', whereby a pupil's minor negative interactions or infringement of rules are ignored and his or her positive interactions are praised. A behavioural contract can also be drawn up between parents, teachers and the pupil stating SMART targets, specific interventions and success criteria. The behavioural approach is more effective when combined with a similar programme at home.

I do my best when I am given a variety of structured activities and rewards for working well!

- **The ecosystemic approach** uses a reframing technique as a way of enabling the pupil and teachers to break out of a cycle of negative interactions. This technique requires teachers to interpret all the pupil's behaviour – including negative behaviour – as having some positive effects. Teachers can suggest to the pupil that his or her negative behaviour may for instance be a way of asking for help or that while the negative behaviour is inappropriate now or in this situation it may be more appropriate at another time or in another situation. Teachers must implement reframing sincerely and convincingly if it is to be effective.

Key points	★ ADD or ADHD
	★ Diagnosis by a doctor or psychiatrist
	★ Diagnosis using DSM IV or ICD 10
	Symptoms
	★ Inattentiveness, impulsivity, hyperactivity
	★ May be associated with learning difficulties, aggression, substance misuse and peer rejection

■ Pupils with anxiety disorder or phobic problems

Introduction

Children and adolescents may be anxious or fearful for a variety of reasons and as a result either avoid school or display emotional difficulties in the classroom. These anxieties or fears may be expressed in different ways within the classroom, for example pupils withdrawing into themselves and being aggressive, phobic or obsessive.

Definition

There are three common disorders: separation anxiety disorder, generalised anxiety disorder and specific phobias. Post-traumatic stress disorder is less common.

- **Separation anxiety** is developmentally inappropriate anxiety resulting from fear of separation or actual separation from parents and others to whom the pupil is closely attached. This problem occurs more frequently in younger children than in adolescents. Such pupils worry that their parents will be harmed, desert them or fail to return home. They also fear that they themselves will be harmed or become separated from their parents. These pupils appear overdependent and wish to stay physically close to their parents. They manifest tearfulness, tantrums or physical illness when they are separated or threatened with separation.

- **Generalised anxiety** occurs where pupils have worries that persist through time but that are not related to any particular thing or event. There may be worries about what has happened in the past and what may happen in the future. The pupil may appear tense, require constant reassurance or complain of feeling ill. This problem occurs more frequently during adolescence.

- **Specific phobias** occur where pupils have an intense fear of a particular object, event or situation, for example animals, darkness or death. Particular phobias are more common at different ages. These phobias lead pupils to either avoid the particular object or situation or to endure it with extreme fearfulness.

- **Post-traumatic stress disorder** (PTSD) occurs where children have experienced or seen disasters, witnessed or experienced physical violence or sexual abuse and been through serious or life-threatening illnesses. For children to be said to be suffering from PTSD they should have continually re-experienced a traumatic incident (nightmares or flashbacks), or avoided objects or situations (pervasive refusal to look after themselves) that remind them of the event or manifest a high arousal level (sleeping problems).

Interventions

Some interventions, such as graded exposure and relaxation techniques, are not ones that teachers are trained in or can use in the classroom context. However, a behavioural approach based on operant conditioning can be useful for teachers to adopt and implement. This can take the form of charts or contingency management which means reinforcing coping behaviours with material or non–material rewards. Behavioural interventions are more effective when combined with similar action by parents in the home. A cognitive approach can also be helpful; this means encouraging anxious or fearful children to make positive self-statements.

Key points	Separation anxiety
	★ Fear of separation from parents/carers
	★ Fear of harm to parents
	★ Fear of desertion
	★ Overdependency
	Generalised anxiety
	★ Unrelated to specific objects, situations or events
	★ General worries about the past or future
	Specific phobias
	★ Fears of specific objects, situations or events
	★ Avoidance
	Post-traumatic stress disorder
	★ Anxiety after witnessing or experiencing disasters, life-threatening illnesses or incidents

■ Pupils with depression

Introduction

Many children can feel sad at particular times in their lives especially if they have experienced a family bereavement, lost a friend or pet, been bullied or fallen ill. Ordinary sadness can develop into depression, where the mood of sadness is intense, persistent and pervasive. In young children depression may be manifested in refusal to attend school and complaints about feeling ill. Depression appears to increase during adolescence.

Definition

Depression sometimes refers to a single phenomenon, a condition of extreme sadness or misery. It sometimes refers to a cluster of phenomena, such as a loss or reduction in feeling pleasure, low self-esteem, hopelessness, suicidal thoughts, restlessness, loss of appetite, reduction in weight and insomnia. It is described as a disorder if the sadness is severe, frequent and persistent. Sometimes other problems occur together with depression, for example a conduct or anxiety disorder, interpersonal difficulties, absenteeism from school. Depressed children often have depressed parents and siblings and live in stressed families. Depression generally increases with age, being more frequent among adolescents than children, girls more than boys. Risk factors are a tendency towards self-blame, low self-esteem, school failure, and rejection by parents and peers.

Interventions

- **Ecosystemic interventions** involve helping adolescents to reframe their maladaptive perceptions of situations by encouraging them to interpret situations more positively. This can be assisted by the use of a diary that helps adolescents to identify irrational or negative thoughts and their connections with mood.

- **Cognitive-behavioural interventions** can take the form of encouraging the adolescent to engage in problem-solving exercises for particular problems, such as social exclusion. Adolescents are encouraged to brainstorm solutions, select one, try it and evaluate the outcome. Coping strategies can be suggested, such as where possible avoiding situations that lead to negative thoughts and eliciting support from peers or adults. Adolescents can also be encouraged to undertake activities that help raise their self-esteem, e.g. by keeping a diary that records positive events, reinforcement and self-reinforcement for positive thoughts and achievements, constructing a self-profile that lists positive qualities, teaching other children.

Key points	★ Bereavement, loss of relationships, physical, sexual and emotional abuse ★ Intensity, persistence and pervasiveness ★ Increases with age, especially during adolescence; girls more than boys ★ Can be associated with conduct and anxiety disorders **Symptoms** ★ Extreme sadness ★ Loss of pleasurable feelings ★ Hopelessness and helplessness ★ Insomnia, loss of appetite and weight **Risk factors** ★ Tendency to self-blame ★ Low self-esteem ★ Depressed parent, rejection by parents or peers ★ School failure, bullied at school

■ Pupils with learning difficulties, including specific learning difficulties

Introduction

Pupils are described as having learning difficulties (LD) if they have a 'significantly greater difficulty in learning than the majority of children of his age', or a 'disability which either prevents or hinders him from making use of educational facilities of a kind generally provided in schools, within the area of the local authority concerned, for children of his age' (Education Act 1981).

Pupils with learning difficulties are often referred for assessment to special educational needs teachers within schools as well as educational psychologists. Recommendations for younger pupils often involve specific, sometimes individual or small-group, skills training in literacy or numeracy. Older pupils also benefit from a clearly differentiated curriculum.

Pupils with a specific learning difficulty (SpLD) are described as having difficulties with aspects of literacy, language or mathematics despite otherwise normal intellectual functioning determined by IQ tests. They have 'significant difficulties ... not typical of their general level of performance' (DfE Code of Practice 1994).

Medical and cognitive models inform theoretical perspectives; there exists a range of assessment methods and teaching materials. There are resource, administrative and legal implications as well as controversies surrounding SpLD and dyslexia.

Definition

The pupil experiencing learning difficulties will display 'significant discrepancies' and will fall behind 'progressively' in comparison with the 'majority of children of his or her age in academic attainment' (DfE Code of Practice 1994).

Learning difficulties can lead to a variety of other compounding difficulties, in particular, behaviour problems. Left undetected, pupil self-esteem may become severely affected, a range of 'challenging' behaviours displayed and task avoidance increased.

Controversy surrounds definitions of specific learning difficulties. Disagreement exists over terminology, subtypes and the interpretation of the data considered central to the differentiation of syndromes such as dyslexia. SpLD is usually considered to be a subset of the learning difficulties category but a lack in the specificity of both concepts predominates. Pupils with specific learning difficulties are generally found to be of average or above-average ability, displaying apparent discrepancies in achievement and error patterns often indicating auditory or visual processing difficulties. Left undetected, pupil self-esteem, behaviour and attitude to work deteriorates. They may attract negative labels such as 'lazy', thus compounding their frustration and adding to their confusion. It is recognised that pupils with SpLD can experience 'severe emotional and behavioural difficulties', and 'difficulties in concentration' (DfE Code of Practice 1994). There is agreement that any learning, emotional or behavioural difficulties are more successfully addressed when identified early.

Interventions

Learning difficulties exist along a continuum: this section illustrates some ideas for good practice which have been shown to benefit pupils of all abilities in the classroom.

Learning and behaviour are significantly affected by pupil self-perception and the expectation pupils have of themselves as learners. Teachers' expectations, based on perception, are equally important factors in determining responses to pupil difficulties and attainment. Learning difficulties, physical impairment, gender, race, appearance, sociability and accent have all been shown to prejudice the teacher. An awareness of expectations and thus self-fulfilling prophecies may be ascertained through the use of the different pro formas in this book (see pp. 94–121) as well as through systematic observation and discussion with pupils.

Peer acceptance has a positive influence on pupil self-esteem while isolated pupils may display either aggressive or withdrawn behaviour. Pupils consistently rejected or ignored by peers may show fearful or anxious behaviour which interferes with the necessary confidence to approach new tasks, take risks and maintain the perseverance necessary for successful learning to take place.

- **Sociometric techniques** can help to identify subgroups, establish which pupils are isolated and which ones are popular or group leaders.

- **Planned groupings** facilitate peer modelling and peer tutoring. This can help to reduce isolation, enhance pupil self-esteem, decrease dependency on the teacher and maximise independent learning.

- Younger pupils can be encouraged during **circletime activities** to value all members of the group. Older pupils can engage in a number of activities designed to improve communication, mutual respect and friendship skills.

- **Peer tutoring** and **cooperative learning** promotes positive interactions between pupils. Pairing the less confident with the more successful for collaborative activities allows both to share success and failure.

- **Team success** promotes individual as well as others' success.

The behavioural perspective emphasises antecedent events when assessing, analysing and changing pupil behaviour. Antecedents within teacher control include the classroom environment and its organisation.

Classroom settings affect pupil responses to teaching and are therefore important factors influencing learning behaviour. Task setting and seating may sometimes take into account pupils' wishes expressing preferences for working alone or in groups.

When planning groups, teachers may also like to consider environmental factors. Pupils are more likely to be focused on tasks when distractions are minimised. Consideration given as to what pupils face may be as important as to whom they face.

- Minimise distractions from windows and doors, ensuring clear visibility to teacher and easy access to necessary equipment.

- Difficult pupils seated near the centre or front of the class are easier for the teacher to attend to or observe.

- Room temperature, time of the day, noise levels and physical space may influence pupil attitude and response to learning.

- Increased pupil choice can facilitate preferences and help to motivate learning.

Pupil response is another factor that can be taken into account.

Pupils may express or demonstrate a preference, strength or weakness for visual, auditory or kinetic learning. Similarly, different methods of teaching appeal to different pupils. Some prefer a discursive approach, some didactic; equally, permissive, authoritarian or democratic teaching stimulate different responses from different pupils.

- Materials offering a variety of responses facilitate pupil preference and choice and allow pupils to work to their strengths.

- Class observation of different sessions will indicate preferred and optimum times for new or intensive learning as well as preferred styles of learning. Taking preferences into account and building in flexibility so that pupil choice can be considered increases possibilities for maximising retention and concentration.

- Practical activities involving motor responses reinforce learning in pupils with kinetic and/or spatial modality preference.

- Teachers sensitive to pupils who do not feel comfortable or confident with public verbal responses can avoid unnecessary conflict and build skills more appropriately during alternative, less threatening situations.

- Awareness of how quickly pupils respond, assimilate and execute their work gives teachers important indications with which to inform the planning, delivery and repetition of tasks.

The behavioural approach emphasises the importance of consequences in influencing behaviour. Elsewhere in this book references are made to the use of positive reinforcement. The identification of a range of effective reinforcers helps ensure that a pupil's learning will increase. Prompting — whether physical, gestural or verbal — is another behavioural technique that can be used to help pupils cope with difficult tasks or remind them of tasks previously learned. The behavioural approach also emphasises objectives-based curricula which include clear targets, task analyses, baselines and success criteria.

Effective learning is increased if pupils are taught to evaluate and reinforce their own learning. Pupils with learning difficulties may have a perception that success is dependent on external factors. All students learn more effectively if they believe that what they contribute to a task makes a difference to the final outcome. Evaluating outcomes enables pupils to recognise the importance of perseverance and effort. Pupils who take some responsibility for their own learning by self-monitoring and charting will feel more motivated and be more able to set and work to realistic targets.

- Emphasising the belief that effort is important and effective nurtures positive self-efficacy, improves the ability to persevere and strengthens the belief that success is possible.

- Pupils can be helped to visualise successful outcomes for themselves and their class.

- Pupils can be encouraged to rehearse and value statements emphasising effort.

- Teachers can ensure that success is experienced with newly acquired learning approaches/skills/strategies.

Decisions made about the size of a teaching group might consider that:

- large groups/whole class are time-efficient;
- in primary or middle schools, whole-class work can prepare pupils for transition to secondary school organisation;
- diverse ability levels are easier to address in smaller groups.

Generally, pupils in larger groupings respond better to:

- shorter instructions, a varied pace of speaking and delivery and the skilful use of questions which involves pupils, encourages active learning and checks for understanding;
- class rules which have been clearly communicated and checked for understanding – these will then have a higher profile and are less likely to be seriously contravened;

- public humour (not sarcasm) – memory is enhanced and teacher–pupil relationships can improve.

In smaller groups, greater consideration can be given to pupils with learning difficulties using:

- multi-sensory methods;
- individualised highly structured skills programmes such as phonological awareness training (PAT) which emphasises the use of rhyme and rhythm in the teaching of literacy skills;
- non-teaching staff for additional support.

Key points	★ Behavioural approach
	★ Objectives-based curriculum
	★ Baseline
	★ Task analysis: breaking down into subtasks
	★ SMART targets
	★ Antecedents and consequences
	★ Behavioural interventions: positive and negative reinforcement, shaping and fading
	★ Cognitive interventions: phonological awareness training
	★ Social learning interventions: modelling
	★ Success criteria

Chapter 5

Special topics

Infant classroom behaviour

Introduction

Infant children's learning and behaviour are influenced by temperament, family and cultural background, parental upbringing, relationships between siblings and, in particular, the negotiation of developmental stages and milestones. Children are often at different stages of development. Behaviour problems can be transitory during this period of development.

Behavioural development

- Children in infant schools can be at different developmental stages.
- They can come to school with different ideas and experiences as to what is acceptable or unacceptable in terms of expression of feelings and behaviour. Their ideas may be influenced by their social and cultural context.
- They may find it difficult to understand their feelings, particularly when they experience two opposite emotions.
- Their attempts at self-control may well be influenced by the ways in which adults react to feelings and behaviour.

Young children are likely to develop emotional and behavioural difficulties if:

- they feel physically and emotionally neglected;
- they are being physically or sexually abused;
- they have parents or carers experiencing psychiatric disorders, e.g. depression;
- they experience family conflicts;
- their parents have separated recently;
- they have not had the opportunity or the space to play;
- they do not have the necessary social and interpersonal skills required to develop positive relationships with other children and adults;
- their level of cognitive development does not enable them to understand the concept of rules along with the need to follow rules.

Strategies that help to prevent emotional and behavioural difficulties are:

- displaying empathy, warmth and acceptance;
- acknowledging feelings;
- providing play space and opportunities for play;
- encouraging helping skills, particularly using mixed-aged groups;
- explaining rules.

We feel nice when we are praised by our teacher!

Behavioural approach

A behavioural approach perceives young children as learning or unlearning behaviour. Behaviour and misbehaviour is seen as resulting from a process of positive or negative reinforcement and also through punishment.

Behaviour can be modified by:

- changing the antecedents or consequences of a given problem behaviour;
- identifying and praising positive behaviour;
- ignoring minor misbehaviour or attention-seeking behaviour while at the same time praising positive behaviour and appropriate requests;
- praising descriptively, i.e. informing the child specifically and precisely what they are doing right;
- reprimanding the child calmly and quietly;
- implementing effective sanctions, e.g. time out from the group or classroom;
- sitting the child with appropriate role models who can help display appropriate behaviour to the child, and using older children to help younger children learn appropriate behaviour;
- modelling the behaviour and getting the child to rehearse the behaviour;

- using external or internal time out, i.e. sending a child out of the classroom or separating the child from the rest of the class;
- using behaviour charts to reward positive behaviour.

Classroom organisation

The teacher should consider the following factors for their possible influence on learning and behaviour in the classroom:

- the physical environment, e.g. decor, ambient noise, temperature and lighting;
- the layout of the classroom, e.g. the seating and grouping of children;
- the location of activities and equipment, particularly for those children with special educational needs;
- the display of rules, instructions and children's work;
- the demonstration of procedures and expectations;
- the visual access to the class as a whole;
- the ways in which parents/carers are incorporated into class activities.

Friendship skills

One of the central aims of a teacher is to encourage children to positively relate to each other as well as to adults. There are various ways in which this can be achieved:

- modelling positive social interactions;
- positively reinforcing prosocial behaviour;
- forming groups that encourage cooperative behaviour;
- using peer tutoring, i.e. encouraging other children who have the appropriate social and learning skills to help other children;
- using children as role models;
- using circle work to develop speaking, listening skills and other social skills;
- using assertiveness training to enable children to stand up for their rights without being aggressive and infringing the rights of other children.

I don't like being left out!

Key interventions	Infant behaviour
	★ Positive reinforcement
	★ Behaviour charts
	★ Modelling
	★ Circle work
	★ Behaviour rehearsal
	★ Peer tutoring
	★ Grouping
	★ Assertiveness training

Streaming and mixed ability

The concept of ability

Streaming and mixed ability raise questions and controversies concerning the nature of intelligence and intelligence testing. These issues relate to how far intelligence is perceived as a unitary and fixed entity, how far it is genetically or environmentally determined and how far it can be adequately assessed through intelligence tests. Teachers may assume in certain cases that intelligence is fixed and unchangeable when in fact it is not. They may also assume that allocation to streams is accurate when it may not be.

Teachers need to consider the influence of mixed ability grouping and streaming on pupils they teach.

General points about streaming

- Low streams tend to have a disproportionate number of boys and pupils from lower socio-economic groups and from ethnic groups.

- Allocation to streams can be rather arbitrary and not altogether based on ability or achievement and therefore children of the same ability may end up being placed in different streams.

- The movement of pupils between streams is often limited and pupils as a consequence may stay in the same stream regardless of their academic progress.

- Teachers may hold negative attitudes, e.g. low expectations towards pupils in low streams, which may end up being communicated to those pupils.

Pupils who are in streamed classes may experience:

- low self-esteem as a result of being placed in low streams, especially where the hierarchy of those streams is apparent to those pupils;

- negative attitudes and low expectations from teachers who dislike teaching such pupils because of their perceived poor behaviour and attitudes towards school.

General points about mixed ability classes

- Mixed ability classes may be streamed in class through subgroups based on ability.

- Lower ability pupils may be seen as difficult, and needing to be contained.

- Teachers tend to teach to an 'average pupil' and as a result neglect the higher and lower ability pupils.

Teaching pupils in streamed and mixed ability classes

In order to avoid or minimise behaviour problems teachers should:

- reflect on their attitude to and expectations of pupils who are in low streams;

- group pupils appropriately within mixed ability classes;

- consider their teaching style and methods in relation to streamed and mixed ability classes, e.g. flexibility, differentiation, a range of audio-visual resources and involvement of pupils in making decisions about their learning.

Key considerations	**Streaming** ★ Concept of 'ability': teacher attitudes and expectations ★ Pupil placement criteria ★ Transfer possibilities ★ Deviant subculture **Mixed ability** ★ Key considerations ★ Balance of 'ability' ★ Flexible teaching methods ★ Differentiation ★ Grouping criteria

Appendix 1

Case study
– a secondary class

This case study is hypothetical. It is an example based on experience in several secondary schools and provides a procedural and analytical account of class-based assessment and intervention. While it honestly reflects a range of interventions, its findings should not be overgeneralised. It is always most important to assess each class individually.

Referral

Referral route

Pastoral Year 9 head and SENCO referred the class of 30 at the beginning of the summer term.

Referral reasons

Noisy, arguments with peers (within classroom setting), un-homogeneous group, poorly established and shifting friendships, slow settling to work, low work output, underachieving, shouting/calling out to teachers, not listening to each other.

Referral background

- New NC Year 9 tutor group: a composite class recently formed (together for two terms) due to a reorganisation of two tutor groups. The group included four pupils new to the school in the past two months. Two were recent permanent exclusions from different neighbouring schools, one had moved from another school through parental choice and one had recently moved into the area.

- Five pupils on the SEN register. One with a statement of special educational needs, two at SEN Stage 1 and two at SEN Stage 2. All pupils listed on SEN register had learning difficulties.

- School pastoral year head and SENCO had examined the seating plan of this class and had suggested regroupings according to results from a questionnaire to pupils asking:
    1. Who do you like to sit with?
    2. Who do you work best with?
    3. Who are your friends in your tutor group?
    4. Who would you choose to organise a class party?
    5. Who do you like to help you with your work?

Assessment

It was agreed important to the success of the intervention that pupils be involved as much as possible in the processes of **assessment, formulation, intervention** and **evaluation**.

Perspectives

Predominantly behavioural and cognitive-behavioural.

Behavioural perspective
- Establish pre-intervention baseline.
- Identify individual and group behaviours.
- Identify behaviour patterns including antecedents and consequences.
- Identify rewarding mechanisms/successful strategies.

Cognitive-behavioural perspective
- Establish pre-intervention baseline.
- Identify individual and group behaviours.
- Attempt to identify cognitive antecedents and consequences.
- Identify rewarding mechanisms/attitudes.
- Assess class motivation to change.
- Assess class's and teacher's attributions, perceptions, attitudes, beliefs and expectations.

Assessment methods

A range of methods contributed to the assessment stage (see the chart opposite).
- Classroom-based observations.
- Individual pupil interviews.
- Discussions with subject teachers and pupils.
- Discussions with pastoral year head and SENCO.
- Questionnaires to subject teachers.
- Questionnaires to pupils.

Assessment details: observation

Fixed interval sampling (FIS) observation schedule
(from: Ayers *et al.* (1996) *Assessing Individual Needs*. London: David Fulton Publishers)

FIS observations indicated the percentages of time or frequency of:
- on/off task, punctuality, settling to work, initial and subsequent task clarification;

	Perspectives, methods of assessment, pro formas and published sources of pro formas	
Methods	**Behavioural perspective**	**Cognitive-behavioural perspective**
	Pro formas	Pro formas
Observations Observation checklists	• Fixed interval sampling observation schedule* • Class/group observation and analysis sheet† • Teacher class management checklist†	Informal
Profiles	• Class/group secondary assessment form† • Class/group secondary score sheet†	• Class/group secondary assessment form† • Class/group secondary score sheet†
Questionnaires	• Pupil class/group questionnaire† • Teacher class/group questionnaire†	• Pupil class/group questionnaire† • Teacher class/group questionnaire†
Interviews	Informal	Informal

* from: Ayers *et al.* (1996) *Assessing Individual Needs*. London: David Fulton Publishers.
† see Appendix 3.

- arguments with pupils/teacher, talking within groups and across classroom;

- pupil-initiated teacher attention for work or behaviour (and how attention was initiated – hands up, calling out, out of seat, etc.);

- teacher-initiated attention, e.g. whether teacher attention was initiated by work- or behaviour-related factors and whether teacher attention was subsequently focused on a pupil, group or class and was directed at work or behaviour.

FIS observations indicated that pupils were mostly punctual to lessons. Some pupils were slower to settle than others but the time taken in settling to a task appeared more related to teacher–class interaction and teacher strategy than to the specific demands of subjects or to specific groups. Times taken to settle varied between four and fifteen minutes. Time spent talking during a 35-minute observation period varied between 10 per cent and 55 per cent. Unsanctioned movement was between 3 per cent and 10 per cent. Talking and unsanctioned movement varied widely across subjects and teachers.

Subjects offering degrees of freedom, such as drama and art, were not necessarily noisier. New groupings appeared to have reduced across-class talking but where it persisted, noise levels were higher and arguing more common. Some pupils put up their hands for teacher attention, others called out. Where 'hands up' was not responded to promptly, pupils began to call out for help. Calling out was responded to by teacher attention in over 60 per cent of subjects observed.

Class/group observation and analysis sheet
(see Appendix 3)

The 'Class/group observation and analysis sheet' emphasised:
- the contexts of class behaviours;
- pupil–pupil and pupil–teacher interactions;
- sanctions and rewards used.

Using this pro forma, it was found that the class would arrive more noisily and take longer to settle after certain lessons, during unstructured activities and in classrooms where not all pupils could see the teacher easily at all times (and vice versa). The most frequent misbehaviours were talking out of turn, arguing, shouting, distracting others, leaving seats and being slow to start work.

Across all subjects observed, the most frequent sanction threatened was detention after class and after school, while the most frequent sanction used was writing negative comments in the class book, keeping the class behind at lunch-time and referral to the head of year.

The most frequent rewards used were positive comments written on pupils' work. Ten per cent of subject teachers used verbal praise to the whole class.

Teacher class management checklist
(see Appendix 3)

The 'Teacher class management checklist' emphasised:
- organisation;
- strategies;
- interactions;
- expectations;
- context of behaviours.

Where pupils were expected to line up outside the classroom before the beginning of the lesson, pupils were generally quieter on entry to the classroom and settled to work more quickly. Where teachers reminded pupils of pre-arranged groupings and communicated task and behavioural expectations emphasising positive expectations, pupils responded with more prompt on-task behaviour.

There were indications of a correlation between pupils being greeted negatively and slow class response to instructions. Teachers who directed their general positive comments about work to the whole class while circulating the room appeared to increase task productivity.

Pupils generally responded to the early warning of sanctions by changing behaviour. Some individuals – none of whom was new to the school – persisted in misbehaviours for longer than others despite warnings of sanctions. Pupils appeared to respond positively to instructions given where some element of small-group choice/organisation was allowed.

Observation confirmed

Teachers increased on-task behaviour when they:

- communicated empathy, warmth, interest and respect (cf. C. Rogers 1969) by using positive body language, making positive comments both to individuals and to the whole class, by greeting the class;
- gave clear instructions for the task, and ensured opportunities for clarification;
- scanned the classroom, pre-empted difficulties and publicly recognised appropriate behaviours (cf. Canter's 'assertive discipline' and Kounin's 'withitness');
- gave adequate time checks and limits (cf. Kounin's 'momentum and smoothness');
- gave warnings of transitions and endings (cf. Kounin's 'momentum and smoothness');
- reviewed previous and current tasks (cf. Ausubel 1963);
- varied pace and activities within a lesson;
- gave reminders of pre-established rules and consequences (cf. B. Rogers 1990);
- moved around the room giving positive attention to task (Canter's 'assertive discipline');
- responded to pupils' requests for help promptly but fairly;
- directed work and behavioural comments to the class rather than to individuals;
- gave positive reinforcement for work and behaviour (cf. Kazdin 1994);
- ensured equipment was accessible and well organised;
- encouraged self-assessment activities;
- allowed/negotiated choices, organisation, rules, consequences.

Teachers increased time spent working quietly if they:

- were skilled in keeping pupils on task;
- repeated and insisted on a 'hands up' rule, ignoring calling out;
- positively reinforced pupils who complied with the 'hands up' rule;
- kept their own voice at a moderate level;
- appeared relaxed;

- waited for silence before giving instructions;
- ignored minor chatting;
- used non-verbal signals to request quiet or a decrease in noise levels;
- positively reinforced (descriptive praise, verbal and written) acceptable levels of talking;
- explicitly allowed times for talking and times for silence.

Pupils settled faster to work if teachers:
- arrived promptly either with or before their pupils;
- emphasised expectations of an orderly entry into the classroom;
- had an established routine at the beginning of the lesson, e.g. calling the register;
- allowed some initial talking time, emphasising that permission had been given/earned;
- gave simple written work at the start of the lesson, e.g. date/title;
- ensured necessary equipment was available and accessible.

Observation also enabled the identification of teachers' own specific successful strategies:
- music teacher used non-verbal cues for silence/attention, e.g. note/chord/phrase on the piano;
- PE teacher used non-verbal cues for attention, e.g. whistle and hand in the air;
- drama teacher used non-verbal cues for silence/attention, e.g. hand in the air;
- form tutor stood with the pupils outside the classroom waiting for them to line up and insisted on silence before entry to classroom;
- history teacher expected pupils to stand behind chairs in silence at beginning of the lesson;
- English teacher set time limits throughout the lesson; often negotiated, they referred to short-, medium- and long-term tasks.

(Also see Appendix 2, Customising pro formas.)

Profiles, interviews and questionnaires – teachers

As well as informal discussion during observation feedback, teachers were asked to complete various pro formas (see the chart on p. 77 and Appendix 3). This was intended both to inform and motivate staff as well as to give data for baselines and later comparison. Teacher time is scarce and so the forms were designed to be simple, for swift completion.

Class/group secondary assessment form and score sheet
(see Appendix 3)

The 'Class/group secondary assessment form and score sheet' emphasised:

- comparisons of teacher perception across subjects;
- categories relating to learning as well as behaviour;
- comparison of behaviour with other classes in the same year;
- prioritising concerns;
- individuals causing concern;
- target setting;
- positives;
- successful strategies already in use.

Collating results from all subject teachers on to the score sheet highlighted considerable variation in teachers' experiences and perceptions of the class. Four subject teachers scored the class low (i.e. below acceptable) across most categories. Categories relating to learning showed greatest consistency where most teachers agreed learning outcomes to be below acceptable and literacy skills to be average. Variation occurred in teachers' perceptions of pupil's attitude towards work where nearly 70 per cent found pupils' attitudes to be a cause for concern yet over 25 per cent reported them to be between acceptable and excellent. Peer group interaction gained consistently low scores between concerned and below acceptable. Variation appeared in perceptions of pupil–staff interactions although most teachers highlighted shouting out as a priority concern. Pupil movement was inconclusive with some teachers noting the category as not appropriate, and other scores ranged from concern to acceptable. Use of equipment was not seen to be a problem although several teachers noted that the same individuals tended to forget equipment on a regular basis. Most teachers felt the class behaviour compared unfavourably with other classes in the year. A common core of pupils causing concern related to learning was identified.

Collation of teachers' concerns prioritised the following areas:

- learning outcomes;
- attitude towards work;
- communication;
- peer interaction;
- interaction with staff;
- class noise.

Positives mentioned included:

- likeable class;
- can produce some good work;

- supportive to new pupils to the class;
- responsive to positives – praise, humour;
- some strong friendships;
- lively class, can be fun to teach.

Strategies mentioned tended to reflect those discussed in observation feedback.

Teacher class/group questionnaire
(see Appendix 3)

A 'Teacher class/group questionnaire' was designed so that data could be gathered about teachers' perceptions, attitudes and experiences of the class. Emphasis was placed on ease of use and speed of completion.

Teachers were encouraged to think about certain statements describing various class attitudes to work and behaviour. Marking responses on a continuum established a baseline and also emphasised the possibility of movement (i.e. improvement) and the relative degrees of severity of the behaviours. Many teachers had lost much of their goodwill for the class and yet were able to describe positive ways in which they wanted it to improve. This suggested to us that teachers would be able to suspend their negativity if they felt the class were working towards similar goals.

Teachers across subject areas generally felt that class orientation to learning was a cause for concern.

They felt there to be a general lack of:

- confidence in beginning new pieces of work;
- perseverance when making mistakes;
- motivation;
- independence;
- care in the presentation of work.

Teachers agreed that the class were able to:

- make appropriate requests for help (although they were often made inappropriately);
- respond to positive reinforcement;
- accept but not immediately respond to correction;
- be cooperative with each other at times.

Interviews and questionnaires – pupils

It was felt that a larger number of pupils would feel more able to engage in a fuller and more frank discussion of views, issues and feelings if they were interviewed individually, in groups and as a class using the 'Pupil questionnaire' and open-ended informal discussion. Time is always a constraint for such in-depth work. However, it was felt that the fullest possible involvement of all pupils was central to both the accuracy of the assessment and to the likelihood of success of the intervention.

Interesting comments followed once initial fears had been allayed that they were not 'in trouble again' when called out in groups for informal discussion.

The class compared themselves unfavourably with other tutor groups in their year who they perceived as being more popular and more successful with the teachers because they were awarded more certificates. There was a general feeling amongst most pupils that they were 'the naughty class of the year ...' and that they 'may as well be known for something'.

Pupil class/group questionnaire
(see Appendix 3)

The 'Pupil class/group questionnaire' focused on the identification of:
- favourite subjects;
- positive/negative aspects of lessons;
- positive aspects of teachers;
- successful teacher strategy;
- identification of subjects where class were perceived as well/badly behaved;
- reasons the class settled quickly to work/behaved well;
- own feelings when the class were behaving badly;
- popular rewards;
- perceptions of how class rewards might be earned;
- class self-perception;
- popular individuals;
- individual targets.

This questionnaire produces copious data which can be followed through on individual and class levels. For the sake of brevity and the purposes of this case study, only a few aspects have been represented in the assessment.

There was a general feeling that most of the teachers did not like the class and that even when they did behave or complete work, no-one cared or noticed. Pupils did name some teachers as exceptions but there was a lack of consistency about this in all but two teachers named. Pupils agreed that the class behaved better when teachers were 'strict' and fair but gave anecdotal examples rather than explanations of their definitions.

Factors listed as reasons for liking teachers were commonly:
- caring;
- friendly;

- mark work regularly;
- helpful;
- sense of humour;
- interesting.

Factors listed as reasons for disliking lessons were commonly:

- pupils are too noisy(!);
- teacher talks for too long;
- teacher does not explain things sufficiently.

Most pupils felt that they were able to settle down quickly when they:

- liked the teacher;
- found the work interesting;
- worked in groups;
- knew how much work they were expected to do in the lesson;
- got lots of help.

Very few pupils stated that they felt as though they had to join in class disruption due to peer pressure, although over 50 per cent admitted that they joined in when others 'mucked about'. Several admitted they thought it was 'a laugh' and so they would join in.

Under 20 per cent thought they would think about ways in which they could help the class to settle down when they were being disruptive.

Pupils said they would like the following if they had worked well:

- good mark written in book;
- letter home praising work;
- teacher to praise work;
- take the work to show to the head of year.

The most popular rewards were stated as:

- class party;
- day off(!);
- class name etched on plaque/trophy;
- choose a video to watch during a lesson;
- class day trip.

Pupils thought that to earn the rewards they would have to:

- stop being noisy;
- always finish their work;
- always do what the teachers asked.

When asked to describe themselves to a newcomer to the class, descriptions most frequently used were:

- noisy;
- unpopular with teachers, disobedient;
- always fighting, bad, horrible;
- friendly, helpful, 'a laugh'.

When asked why they had been chosen to complete the questionnaire, most classes gave negative reasons. This is often a good starting point in formulation with pupils and allows the suggestion that they may have been chosen because their teachers thought they were special enough to get some extra attention. Other explanations follow naturally such as teachers wanting to raise pupils' levels of achievement and a desire to improve their relationships.

Our experience has been that in most cases pupils are pleasantly surprised and, although a few cynics usually express some doubt, a more positive attitude has generally begun to be engendered.

Formulation

Assessment information was distributed and fully discussed with subject teachers and a consensual agreement reached regarding general **predisposing**, **precipitating** and **perpetuating** causes for the difficult class behaviours. Some of these factors are shown in the table below.

Factors	Behavioural
Predisposing	• Lack of consistent teacher strategy • Lack of certainty about class rules • Lack of success (pupil and teacher) • Disorganised classroom
Precipitating	• Negative comments from teacher • Teacher arrives late to lesson • Disinterest in work • Confusion about the task set • Long-winded explanations • Previous lesson ended badly/late
Perpetuating	• Lack of positive reinforcement for desired behaviours • Positive reinforcement for undesired behaviours • Lack of rewards • Unsuccessful strategies repeatedly used

Identifying successful strategies used by various subject teachers encouraged both public and private reflection on which strategies worked as well as those found to be counter-productive. As far as was possible, the feedback was anonymous.

It was agreed that there was a general lack of consistency in the enforcement and reinforcement of basic class rules. It was also agreed that there was a general lack of positive reinforcement, particularly directed at the whole class and especially public. Teachers maintained, however, that 'the class did not deserve any reinforcement', which gave some indication about confusion that existed between the concepts of reinforcement and reward.

Cognitive-behavioural approach	
Activating events – precursors	**Beliefs – cognitive processes**
• Lack of praise/reward • Negative comments • Poor explanations	• 'We never succeed' • 'We're no good' • 'Teachers don't like us' • 'We must be stupid'

Teachers were particularly interested in learning about the class self-perception and showed surprised at the pupils' words: 'We may as well be well known for being the naughty class of our year, we don't get certificates or anything else. We've got to be known for something.'

Assessment information was discussed with pupils who were equally surprised to find out that teachers did have some positive views about them. Although they seemed to agree that they were slow to settle to work, talked too much and tended to argue amongst themselves, they were not able to take on responsibility for their behaviours; they did not really believe they could help themselves change.

Formulation summary

It became clear to all concerned that both pupils and teachers were locked unnecessarily in a self-perpetuating and negative cycle of behaviours. Both teachers and pupils had lost much goodwill, patience and expectation of anything positive happening. Neither were adept at pleasing the other and both sides were feeling disenchanted, deskilled and disliked by the other. While teachers and pupils seemed to recognise what desired behaviours each of them should perform, neither had much idea of where or how to begin to change entrenched beliefs and behaviour patterns. Both teachers and pupils tended to minimise their achievements and maximise negative aspects of themselves. It was interesting to see how far they shared the same cognitive distortions.

The process of assessment had begun to introduce a little optimism, but there was a need to agree simple targets and introduce specific strategies that would be consistently applied by all staff.

Intervention

Teachers

Teachers were called to a meeting where the following were discussed and agreed:

- details of the assessment and formulation;
- prioritise four desired behaviours;
- adopt certain strategies to reinforce the desired behaviours;
- consistency;
- success criteria;
- a system of monitoring progress;
- a final class reward.

Pupils were seen during a tutor group lesson where the following were discussed and agreed:

- details of the assessment and formulation;
- prioritise four desired behaviours (same as those set by teachers – in fact there was a remarkable correlation);
- how to maintain the four desired behaviours (some modelling and rehearsal took place);
- success criteria;
- a system of monitoring progress;
- a final class reward.

The four target behaviours were:

1. to quietly line up outside the classroom before entry with teacher;
2. to put hands up to gain teacher attention;
3. to complete all work set to best ability during the lesson;
4. to respond to teacher instruction promptly.

Agreed teacher strategies were:

- to regularly remind pupils of the class rules and rewards system;
- to wait with pupils lining up outside the classroom;
- to encourage and wait for silence before bringing them into the classroom;
- to call the register at the beginning of the lesson;
- to have a simple written activity ready at the start of the lesson;
- as much as possible, to use non-verbal signals to gain attention/reduce noise.

Implementation and monitoring

It was agreed that the class would be rewarded by a class party when they had gained and maintained an improvement over a period of six weeks. During an art lesson, the whole class became involved in making a huge wall display of two speakers for their tutor room. In liaison with the music department they went on to make a series of musical notes and clefs cut out from coloured cardboard. Each subject teacher was given a stock of musical notes – these were colour coded according to the subject. When the class managed to succeed in achieving a minimum of three targets in a lesson, they were awarded with a musical note. A different pupil was given responsibility each day for collecting and carrying the musical notes and delivering them to the form tutor.

Musical notes were stuck onto the speakers displayed on the classroom wall. Every time ten notes were gained, the form tutor awarded the class with a clef which was stuck around the speakers. It was agreed that there had to be at least one clef for each pupil if the whole class was to have a party.

It soon became apparent in which subjects pupils were succeeding more frequently. Ongoing discussions about progress took place in tutor time and both the form tutor and head of year gave encouragement and support, visiting those subject lessons where less progress was being made. Reminders about goals were reiterated and subject teachers encouraged to observe colleagues' lessons. All subject teachers were encouraged to come into the tutor room to look at the display and encourage the class. This proved exceptionally popular and made a great impact in subject areas where the class were doing less well.

Issues

- Supply teachers were not always reached in time to explain routines and reward systems.

- There was a lack of positive feedback for teachers and their only reward was improved class behaviour.

- Parents were not sufficiently/formally involved.

- Some teachers resented the time and attention given to the 'problem'.

Evaluation

After six weeks:

- time spent on task in most lessons was above 70 per cent;

- unsanctioned talking was reduced to less than 20 per cent;

- teachers perceived less arguing among pupils;

- entry to class and settling to work was acceptable in 60 per cent of subjects taught;

- teachers reported feeling more confident in managing the class;

- pupils reported that they thought the teachers were 'more friendly' (we thought this was partly a result of teachers visiting the pupils' tutor group class);

- teachers reported using some of the strategies with other classes;

- teachers reported using additional strategies discussed during the assessment stage;

- both pupils and teachers reported that they felt more positive about each other.

It is always difficult to be exact about evaluation. Unfortunately there was not time to reassess using many of the original pro formas. However, observations were made by staff in the school which had the dual advantage of collective comparative data and seeing a colleague at work.

The most useful elements to the intervention were that colleagues learnt from and began to support each other, and in doing so they grew in expertise, confidence and began to minimise the teacher isolation often experienced by teachers in schools – that the skills were transferable was a bonus. The class changed from one renowned for disruption to one known for the fantastic wall display, which of course other classes and teachers saw when using the tutor room. The self-esteem of both pupils and teachers had been improved.

Appendix 2

Customising pro formas

Introduction

The forms at the back of this book (Appendix 3) are intended to be used by teachers too busy to design their own. However, designing a pro forma with a colleague will often meet your requirements more exactly than those predesigned. For this reason we urge you both to customise the prepared pro formas where desired but also to look at the following two skeletal suggestions for forms mentioned in the case study and consider how they may be of use to you.

Teacher strategy checklist

Observing colleagues in the classroom can be a very instructive and supportive exercise. Before a class is observed, if teacher(s) are given the opportunity to study a strategy checklist the range of positive strategies included may be noted for future incorporation. This process is enhanced and may feel less threatening if both observer and class teacher collaborate in devising a list together beforehand.

Specific feedback of positive consequences enables teachers to link their strategies with positive outcomes in class behaviour. This is often useful where a teacher is unconscious of something they are doing well!

Highlighting alternative strategies alongside observation feedback can increase the probability of future trialling of a broader range of strategies. Successful strategies not included on the observation schedule are also noted for feedback.

An observation checklist is not intended to be exhaustive, but seeks to identify objective descriptions of existing good practice.

Some considerations for a checklist

Which teacher strategies might support the following?

- *A positive classroom ethos* (C. Rogers) – communicates empathy, warmth, genuineness.
- *Congruent communication* (H. Ginott) – acknowledges feelings, invites cooperation, solution-focused thinking.
- *No-lose conflict resolution* (T. Gordon) – collaborative rule setting.
- *A classroom discipline plan* (B. Rogers) – assertive discipline approaches.
- *Democratic teaching* (R. Dreikurs) – characterised as friendly, encouraging, collaborative, helpful, willing to share responsibility, development of pupil self-discipline.
- *Vigilance* (J. Kounin) – desists, 'withitness', momentum and smoothness, group alerting and accountability, overlapping, valence, challenge arousal.
- *Reinforcement* (B. F. Skinner) – constant, intermittent, positive, negative.

Teacher class/group questionnaire

Keeping categories clear and simple to mark make completing a pro forma easier and quicker.

Using a continuum (such as in the class/group assessment forms) allows busy teachers to circle a number and allows for scoring on to a sheet which can be used again at a later date to show progress.

Descriptive words such as 'concern', 'acceptable' and 'excellent' allow for later comparison and aid swift assessment.

A 'Teacher class/group questionnaire' would be designed to facilitate teacher reflection on the management of learning and behaviour in the classroom. The following categories might be considered when designing such a questionnaire.

Class orientation to learning

- reading;
- speaking and listening;
- writing;
- confidence;
- perseverance;
- motivation;
- independence;
- settling to work;
- presentation.

Class orientation to teachers

- appropriate requests for help;
- responding to positive reinforcement;
- immediate acceptance of correction;
- immediate acceptance of instruction;
- cooperation.

Pupils presenting learning/emotional or behavioural problems

'Underline the descriptors which indicate the ways the class relate to you:

Friendly/Hostile/Aggressive/Caring/Helpful/Responsive/Other'

Class orientation to peers

- cooperation;
- collaboration;
- conflict;
- social/ethnic/gender mixing.

'Underline the following descriptors which indicate the ways in which you would like the class to change:

Cooperative/Helpful/Responsive/Collaborative/...'

Appendix 3

Class management forms

Teacher/class cognitive planning guide and sheet (pp. 94–5)

This is a guide to be used as a structure to enable teachers to plan an assessment and formulation based on a cognitive-behavioural perspective. It can be used for any age of pupil able to articulate their own ideas about their difficulties.

Class/group primary assessment form (pp. 96–7)

This form is intended for use with primary classes/groups. It emphasises: comparisons of teacher perception across subjects; categories relating to learning as well as behaviour; comparison of behaviour with other classes in the same year; prioritising concerns; individuals causing concern; target setting; context; positives; successful strategies already in use.

Class/group primary score sheet (p. 98)

This score sheet is intended to be used with the class/group primary assessment form. It allows scores to be recorded several times over a chosen period of time, thus showing improvement or deterioration over time. It is very useful in class assessments.

Class/group secondary assessment form (pp. 99–100)

This form is intended for use with secondary classes/groups, and emphasises the same categories as the 'Class/group primary assessment form'.

Class/group secondary score sheet (p. 101)

This score sheet is intended to be used with the 'Class/group secondary assessment form'. Scoring categories on this sheet allows an instant visual comparison across subjects. It is very useful in class assessments.

Teacher class management checklist (pp. 102–5)

This form can be used to record information and observations on the organisation and interactions of a class and their teacher(s). It is very useful in class assessments.

Class/group observation and analysis sheet (pp. 106–7)

This form can be used to record information and observations on the behaviour of a particular class, form or group in a primary or secondary context. It is very useful in class assessments.

Class/form ABC sheet (p. 108)

This form can be used for any age group. It may be used as an observation schedule or a recording sheet for a functional analysis of class/group behaviour.

Primary (junior) class/group questionnaire (pp. 109–14)

This questionnaire is useful in gauging the perceptions, beliefs and attitudes of pupils. It focuses on a wide range of topics and is best completed with a teacher present to read and explain completion. Anonymity should always be assured wherever possible.

Secondary class/group questionnaire (pp. 115–19)

This questionnaire is very similar to the one described above but has been adapted for use by older pupils.

Classroom discipline plan (pp. 120–1)

This form can be used as a structure to enable teachers to formulate a class discipline plan. It can be used for any age group.

TEACHER / CLASS COGNITIVE PLANNING GUIDE

ASSESSMENT STAGE

* **DESCRIBE** class / form / group behaviour problem

|||➡ *Ask class for their descriptions - verbal / written*   **Class questionnaire**

|||➡ *Ask teacher(s) for their descriptions - verbal / written*   **Teacher questionnaire**
                                                    Class assessment form
    Class management checklist
    Class ABC form

CONSIDER: latency, frequency, duration, intensity, attitudes, expectations

---

EXAMPLE:

CLASS description: We spend a lot of time chatting in most lessons and don't settle down very quickly.

TEACHER description: Every lesson the class takes ten minutes to get their books and equipment out of their bags and are very noisy for the whole lesson. They generally disregard teacher's instructions and do not expect any consequences.

FORMULATION STAGE

* **CAUSE or REASONS** for the problem **OCCURRING** and **CONTINUING**

|||➡ *Ask class for their ideas about the causes / reasons for the problem*

|||➡ *Ask class for their ideas about the causes / reasons for the problem*

CONSIDER: 3 P's : PREDISPOSING, PRECIPITATING & PERPETUATING cognitions.

EXAMPLE: **Class formulation:**

PREDISPOSING: the class say they are bottom stream / set and therefore are not good at learning

PRECIPITATING: the class say when they are asked to do written work at the beginning of the lesson they take their time because they find it too difficult

PERPETUATING: the class say the teacher is always making negative criticisms of their class so they talk noisily among themselves

---

TEACHER / CLASS COGNITIVE PLANNING SHEET

INTERVENTION STAGE

* **DESCRIBE What the TEACHER can do:**

3 SMART TARGETS

||||➡

||||➡

||||➡

* **DESCRIBE What the CLASS can do:**

3 SMART TARGETS

||||➡

||||➡

||||➡

IMPLEMENTATION

CONSIDER:

✔ **WHO else will be involved?**
EG: Parents / carers / non-teaching staff / Year head

✔ **HOW will progress be MONITORED?**
EG: Class day book /monitoring chart / monitoring book

✔ **HOW will progress / improvement be ACKNOWLEDGED / REWARDED?**
EG: Class rewards based on responses from **Class questionnaire**

✔ **SUCCESS CRITERIA**

REVIEW DATE (S) ☐ ☐ ☐

CLASS / GROUP PRIMARY ASSESSMENT FORM

NUMBER on CLASS REGISTER [ ] **CLASS** [ ] **ETHNICITY**

NUMBER on SEN REGISTER [ ] **TEACHER** [ ]

ESWI / Afro Carib.
Chinese / Somali
Indian / Pakistani
Bengali Other

GENDER RATIO % M / F: [ ]

> Please consider the group / class AS A WHOLE when scoring the following categories.
> Refer to your experience with this group / class over the PAST 4 - 6 WEEKS and circle each
> continuum accordingly. You may choose to underline certain statements or to add your own.

1) Punctuality

1	2	3	4	5
Concern		Acceptable		Excellent

2) Attendance

1	2	3	4	5
Concern		Acceptable		Excellent

3) Literacy

1	2	3	4	5
Concern		Acceptable		Excellent

4) Numeracy

1	2	3	4	5
Concern		Acceptable		Excellent

5) Learning outcomes

1	2	3	4	5
Concern		Acceptable		Excellent

Insufficient work, Unfinished work, Poor quality work
Underachieving, Homework

6) Attitude towards work

1	2	3	4	5
Concern		Acceptable		Excellent

Refusal to work, Starting work, Finishing work
Lack of equipment, Misuse of equipment,

7) Communication

1	2	3	4	5
Concern		Acceptable		Excellent

Listening, Speaking, Discussion

8) Peer / Group interaction

1	2	3	4	5
Concern		Acceptable		Excellent

Unfriendly, Uncollaborative, Uncooperative
Verbal / Physical aggression

9) Interaction with staff

1	2	3	4	5
Concern		Acceptable		Excellent

Rudeness, Shouting out, Refusal to work,
Refusal to move, Verbal / Physical aggression

10) Class noise

1	2	3	4	5
Concern		Acceptable		Excellent

Singing, Laughing, Shouting, Burping, Tapping
Banging, Coughing, Crying, Whistling

11) Pupil movement

1	2	3	4	5

Concern   Acceptable   Excellent

Walking about, Interference with others
Leaving classroom, Barging into others

12) Use of equipment

1	2	3	4	5

Concern   Acceptable   Excellent

Misuse: materials, equipment, furniture, graffiti
Damage: materials, equipment, furniture, vandalism
Failure to bring equipment

13) Context

1	2	3	4	5

Concern   Acceptable   Excellent

Playground, Assembly hall, Gym, Corridors, Mat
Wendy house, Classroom, School journey

14) Group / Class behaviour comparison with other groups/classes

1	2	3	4	5

Concern   Acceptable   Excellent

15) Please list pupils persistently causing concern:

16) Please prioritise and briefly describe 3 areas of concern:
a)

b)

c)

17) Please state three targets for this group / class:
a)

b)

c)

18) Additional information - including POSITIVES.

19) Please list any STRATEGIES undertaken with this group / class.

Please return this form to:

Primary Score Sheet

Class / Group

	1's or 2's
1 Punctuality	
2 Attendance	
3 Literacy	
4 Numeracy	
5 Learning outcomes	
6 Attitude towards work	
7 Communication	
8 Peer group interaction	
9 Interaction with staff	
10 Class noise	
11 Pupil movment	
12 Use of equipment	
13 Context	
14 Group / class behaviour	

1's or 2's

CLASS / GROUP SECONDARY ASSESSMENT FORM

FORM ▢   **NUMBER on REGISTER** ▢   **GENDER RATIO** | % F / M:

SUBJECT ▭

ETHNICITY | ESWI / Afro Carib. / Chinese Somali / Indian / Pakistani Bengali / Other

TEACHER ▭

> Please consider the group / class AS A WHOLE when scoring the following categories. Refer to your experience with this group / class over the PAST 4 - 6 WEEKS and circle each continuum accordingly. You may choose to <u>underline certain statements</u> or to add your own.

1) Punctuality

| 1 | 2 | 3 | 4 | 5 |
Concern   Acceptable   Excellent

2) Attendance

| 1 | 2 | 3 | 4 | 5 |
Concern   Acceptable   Excellent

3) Literacy

| 1 | 2 | 3 | 4 | 5 |
Concern   Acceptable   Excellent

4) Numeracy

| 1 | 2 | 3 | 4 | 5 |
Concern   Acceptable   Excellent

5) Learning outcomes

| 1 | 2 | 3 | 4 | 5 |
Concern   Acceptable   Excellent

Insufficient work, Unfinished work, Poor quality work
Underachieving, Homework

6) Attitude towards work

| 1 | 2 | 3 | 4 | 5 |
Concern   Acceptable   Excellent

Refusal to work, Starting work, Finishing work
Lack of equipment, Misuse of equipment

7) Communication

| 1 | 2 | 3 | 4 | 5 |
Concern   Acceptable   Excellent

Listening, Speaking, Discussion

8) Peer / Group interaction

| 1 | 2 | 3 | 4 | 5 |
Concern   Acceptable   Excellent

Unfriendly, Uncollaborative, Uncooperative
Verbal / Physical aggression

9) Interaction with staff

| 1 | 2 | 3 | 4 | 5 |
Concern   Acceptable   Excellent

Rudeness, Shouting out, Refusal to work,
Refusal to move, Verbal / Physical aggression

10) Class noise

| 1 | 2 | 3 | 4 | 5 |
Concern   Acceptable   Excellent

Singing, Laughing, Shouting, Burping, Tapping
Banging, Coughing, Crying, Whistling

11) Pupil movement

1	2	3	4	5

Concern   Acceptable   Excellent

Walking about, Interference with others
Leaving classroom, Barging into others

12) Use of equipment

1	2	3	4	5

Concern   Acceptable   Excellent

Misuse: materials, equipment, furniture, graffiti
Damage: materials, equipment, furniture, vandalism
Failure to bring equipment

13) Group / Class behaviour comparison with other groups/classes in the year.

1	2	3	4	5

Concern   Acceptable   Excellent

14) Please list pupils persistently causing concern:

15) Please prioritise and briefly describe 3 areas of concern:

*

*

*

16) Please state three targets for this group / class:

*

*

*

17) Additional information - including POSITIVES.

18) Please list any STRATEGIES undertaken with this group / class.

Please return this form to:

Secondary Score Sheet

Class / Form / Group	1 Pn	2 At	3 Lt	4 Nm	5 Lo	6 Aw	7 Cm	8 Pg	9 Is	10 Cn	11 Pm	12 Ue	13 Gc	1's or 2's
MATHEMATICS														
ENGLISH														
SCIENCE														
TECHNOLOGY														
HISTORY														
GEOGRAPHY														
LANGUAGES														
RELIGIOUS EDUCATION														
P.E. / GAMES														
ART														
MUSIC														
DRAMA														
INFORMATION TECHNOLOGY														
P.S.H.E.														
1's or 2's														

TEACHER CLASS MANAGEMENT CHECKLIST

This form can be used to RECORD INFORMATION and OBSERVATIONS on the ORGANISATION and INTERACTIONS of a CLASS and their TEACHER(S).   Tick, circle or underline as desired.

CLASS/GROUP/FORM:	TEACHER:	TIME:

Beginning of lesson

PUNCTUALITY

Teacher arrival	*Before pupils*	*With pupils*	*After pupils*
Pupil arrival	*All on time*	*Most on time*	*Several late*
Teacher response	*Positive reinforcement:* *Negative reinforcement:* *Punishment:*	*verbal / non- verbal / tokens / other* *verbal / non- verbal / other* *warned / given* *verbal / non- verbal / other* *immediate / delayed*	

LINING UP & ENTRY

Location	*Playground*	*Outside class*	*Inside class*
Sequence	*Pre-arranged* *Pre-agreed with pupils* *Teacher direction*	*Arranged in-situ* *Agreed in-situ* *Pupil choice*	
Teacher response	*Positive reinforcement:* *Negative reinforcement:* *Punishment:*	*verbal / non- verbal / tokens / other* *descriptive praise / acknowledgement* *verbal / non- verbal / other* *warned / given* *verbal / non- verbal / other* *immediate / delayed*	

GREETINGS

Initiated by	*Teacher*	*Non-teaching staff*	*Pupils*
Between	*Teacher & group / class* *Non-teaching staff & group /class* *Pupils & teacher*	*Teacher & individual pupils* *Non-teaching staff & individual pupils* *Pupils & non-teaching staff*	

  From *Classroom Management* – © 1998 Harry Ayers and Francesca Gray – David Fulton Publishers

SEATING

Position	Grouped	Rows	Pairs	Individually	Other

Allocation	Pre-arranged Pre-agreed with pupils Teacher direction	Arranged in-situ Agreed in-situ Pupil choice

Teacher response	Positive reinforcement: Negative reinforcement: Punishment:	verbal / non- verbal / tokens / other descriptive praise / acknowledgement verbal / non- verbal / other warned / given verbal / non- verbal / other

COATS & BAGS

Location	Back of / under seats	Coat hooks inside / outside classroom Lockers inside / outside classroom

Reminders	Requested once directly to whole class / to individuals

Teacher response	Positive reinforcement: Negative reinforcement: Punishment:	verbal / non- verbal / tokens / other descriptive praise / acknowledgement verbal / non- verbal / other warned / given verbal / non- verbal / other immediate / delayed

EQUIPMENT

Pupil's	Checked	Sufficient
School's	Accessible	Sufficient

Teacher response	Positive reinforcement: Negative reinforcement: Punishment:	verbal / non- verbal / tokens / other descriptive praise / acknowledgement verbal / non- verbal / other warned / given verbal / non- verbal / other immediate / delayed

REGISTER:

Timing	Beginning of lesson	During lesson	End of lesson

Method	Teacher calls names requiring pupils to respond verbally Teacher scans class / group checking pupil presence

Pupil noise	Acceptable	Unacceptable

INSTRUCTION:

Timing	Beginning of lesson Given when pupils silent	During lesson When mostly silent	End of lesson When pupils noisy
Clarification	Instructions reinforced Initiated by teacher without pupil prompting By teacher at pupil request By pupil (s) at request of teacher		
Activity	Single	Multiple	Open-ended
Organisation	Teacher directed Negotiated with pupils Opportunities for pupil choice		
Expectations	Communicated overtly Time limits for work set / negotiated / reminders given		

Middle of Lesson

Transitions	Warnings given ahead of transition Varied pace Smooth Dead time Noisy Excessive pupil movement		
Vigilance	Scanning classroom Monitoring individual / group work Marking individual / group work Teacher movement around classroom		

PUPIL NOISE:

Levels	Beginning: Middle: End:	Acceptable Acceptable Acceptable	Unacceptable Unacceptable Unacceptable
Expectations	Teacher directed Negotiated with pupils Talking allowed - conditional / unconditional Talking allowed - with time limit / without time limit Silence required by teacher - conditional / unconditional Silence required by teacher - with time limit / without time limit		
Strategies	Requested once directly to whole class / to individuals - Verbal / non verbal Several reminder (s) to whole class / to individuals - Verbal / non verbal		
Teacher response	Positive reinforcement: Negative reinforcement: Punishment:	verbal / non- verbal / tokens / other descriptive praise / acknowledgement verbal / non- verbal / other warned / given verbal / non- verbal / other immediate / delayed	

        From *Classroom Management* – © 1998 Harry Ayers and Francesca Gray – David Fulton Publishers

End of Lesson

EQUIPMENT

Reminders
Tidied away   -   with / without teacher prompt
Requested once directly to whole class / to individuals
Requests repeated to whole class / to individuals

Teacher response

Positive reinforcement:	verbal / non- verbal / tokens / other
	descriptive praise / acknowledgement
Negative reinforcement:	verbal / non- verbal / other
Punishment:	warned / given
	verbal / non- verbal / other
	immediate / delayed

SUMMARY

Overview

Work / behaviour focus	Class / individual focus
Review of lesson by teacher	Reference made to next stage of work
Review of lesson by pupil (s)	

Teacher response

Positive reinforcement:	verbal / non- verbal / tokens / other
	descriptive praise / acknowledgement
Negative reinforcement:	verbal / non- verbal / other
Punishment:	warned / given
	verbal / non- verbal / other
	immediate / delayed

HOMEWORK

Method   Communicated verbally / board / handout

Organisation   Teacher directed   Negotiated with pupils   Opportunities for pupil choice

Timing   Given when pupils silent   When mostly silent   When pupils noisy

Time allowed for teacher explanation   Time allowed for pupil questioning
Time allowed for pupil recording

Clarification   Instructions reinforced
Initiated by teacher without pupil prompting
By teacher at pupil request   By pupil (s) at request of teacher

Expectations   Communicated overtly
Time limits for work set / negotiated / reminders given

LEAVING CLASSROOM

Pupil departure   Orderly   Disorderly

Additional comments:

From Classroom Management – © 1998 Harry Ayers and Francesca Gray – David Fulton Publishers

CLASS / GROUP OBSERVATION & ANALYSIS SHEET

This form can be used to RECORD INFORMATION and OBSERVATIONS on the behaviour of a particular CLASS, FORM or GROUP in a PRIMARY or SECONDARY context. Underline, tick or circle where appropriate.

SCHOOL / UNIT:

CLASS:　　　　　　　**FORM:**　　　　　　　**GROUP:**

Date:　　　　　　　　　　　　**Day:**

Time:　　　　　　　　　　　　**Period:**

CURRENT SUBJECT:　　*Maths / English / Science / Technology / Geography / History Art /Languages / Music / PE / RE / Drama / IT / Other*

CURRENT ACTIVITY:　　*Individual / Group / Class / Open ended / Structured Literacy based / Numeracy based / Other*

WORK / TASK:　　*Differentiation - Delivery Y/N Materials Y/N Outcome Y/N Textbook / Worksheet / Oral / Experiment / Computer Physical / Creative / Practical / Other*

PREVIOUS SUBJECT:　　*Maths / English / Science / Technology / Geography / History Art / Languages / Music / PE / RE / Drama / IT / Other*

TEACHER (S): Current lesson -
　　　　　　　　　Previous lesson -

ENVIRONMENT:　　*Classroom / workshop / lab / gym / studio / playground computer room / theatre / other.*

Environment description:

Temperature: needs to be cooler / hotter
Seating: rows / tables / benches / carpet / other.
Lighting: needs to be increased
Walls: displays / notice-boards / posters / current work
Noise: external source - from other classrooms / playground / street
Field of view - teacher: clear / obstructed - pupils: clear / obstructed
Movement: easy / obstructed

GROUPING　　*Physical - Tables / benches - rows / grouped*
　　　　　　　Grouping - Streaming / Banding / Setting / Mixed Ability

　　　　From *Classroom Management* – © 1998 Harry Ayers and Francesca Gray – David Fulton Publishers

COMPOSITION:

Streamed / Banded / Set / Mixed ability / Other
Mixed / Single sex; Girls / Boys
No. Pupils SEN register: Stages 1- 5 ....
No. of E2L pupils ....
Ethnicity (underline):
ESWI / Afro-Caribbean / Bengali / Indian / Turkish / Greek / Somali / Moroccan / Other

---

ENTRY: *Orderly / Disorderly / Quiet / Noisy / Early / Late / On time / Other*

EXIT: *Orderly / Disorderly / Quiet / Noisy / Early / Late / On time / Other*

BEHAVIOURS:

Pupil - Pupil interaction:

Talking / Arguing / Shouting / Swearing / Cussing / Laughing / Making noises /Distracting others / Throwing things / Threatening / Fighting / Gestures
Interfering with others / Racist / Inappropriate physical contact / Sexist / Bullying / Staring / Spitting / Other

Pupil - Teacher interaction:

Arguing / Shouting / Swearing / Cussing / Laughing / Making noises   / Clings
Throwing things / Threatening / Physical assault / Gestures / Disobeys / Mimic
Spitting / Racist / Inappropriate physical contact / Sexist / Yawning / Other

Other:

Leaving seat / Arriving late / Leaving school / Damaging property / Slow to start work
Writing on property / Withdrawn / Without equipment / Eating / Drinking / Feigns illness
Lighting fire / Indecent exposure / Sighing / Staring / Crying / Yawning

---

SANCTIONS: *Reprimand / Detention / Lines / Referral to HOY / SMT / Report / Other*

REWARDS: *Verbal praise / Positive comments on work / Letters home / Certificates*
Points / Trophies / Journeys / Party / Other

COMPARING CLASS / GROUP BEHAVIOUR:

Across Year	*Better than all*	*Better than most*	*Better than some*
	Worse than all	*Worse than most*	*Worse than some*
Across School			
	Better than all	*Better than most*	*Better than some*
	Worse than all	*Worse than most*	*Worse than some*

Teacher completing sheet:

CLASS / FORM ABC SHEET

DATE / TIME	ANTECEDENTS		BEHAVIOUR	CONSEQUENCES
	DISTANT	IMMEDIATE		

PRIMARY (JUNIOR) CLASS / GROUP QUESTIONNAIRE

SCHOOL [ ]   **DATE** [ ]

PUPIL [ ]   **CLASS** [ ]

This questionnaire is to help your teacher plan work and activities for you. It is a chance for you to say what you think. Please think carefully about your answers and try to complete all of them.
Thank you.

1.   Here is a list of some of the things you do in class.

PUT A CIRCLE around the TWO which you enjoy most:

NUMBER WORK   READING   SCIENCE   GEOGRAPHY   STORY WRITING

DRAMA   PAINTING   MAKING THINGS   COMPUTER   GYM

DRAWING   STORY TIME   HISTORY   MUSIC

2a.   CHOOSE ONE and write it inside the circle: ⁗➤ ⁗➤ ⁗➤

2b.   WHAT do YOU like about this lesson?   Put a circle around the things you like about it.

The KIND of work   The AMOUNT of work   The LEVEL of work

The pupils you SIT next to   The pupils you WORK with

The TEACHER:

Likes us / Friendly / Interesting / Funny / Strict / Fair / Helpful

Gives us stickers / Puts lots of ticks on our work / Puts our work on the wall

Gives us lots of different things to do / Writes nice things on our work

3b. What do you think your group / class DISLIKES about some of the things you do in class?

PUT A CIRCLE AROUND some of the things YOU THINK they dislike.

TOO MUCH reading   Work too HARD   Work is TOO EASY

Teacher doesn't tell us HOW TO DO THINGS

Too much WRITING   Too much HOMEWORK

READING is too hard   Pupils need MORE HELP   Pupils are TOO NOISY

We DON'T UNDERSTAND the work   NOT ENOUGH reading

Teacher TALKS to us for TOO LONG

4. What DO YOU THINK makes your group/class BEHAVE WELL in different lessons?

✔ TICK THE BOXES that show what you think. (You may like to write in 2 lessons of your own.)

Things that make our group / class behave well in lessons.							
✔	Number work ✎	Story writing ✎	Making things ✎	Science ✎	Painting ✎	.... ✎	.... ✎
We like the teacher							
The teacher is fair							
The teacher likes us							
We like the activity							
We can do the work OK							
Lots of time to finish work							
We get lots of help							
Have to stay in our seats							

          From *Classroom Management* – © 1998 Harry Ayers and Francesca Gray – David Fulton Publishers

5. ✔ TICK any of these other things that YOU THINK make your class SETTLE DOWN ✔
QUICKLY to work and to BEHAVE well.

a) We find the work interesting .... ☐

b) We do lots of writing in our book .... ☐

c) We don't have to write anything . ... ☐

d) We work in groups .... ☐

e) We work on our own .... ☐

f) We know how much work our teacher expects us to get done in the lesson .... ☐

i) You are allowed to move freely around in some of the lesson .... ☐

6. When your class is MUCKING ABOUT and the TEACHER IS TRYING TO TEACH the class,
how do YOU USUALLY FEEL:

a) This is a good laugh, I think I'll join in .... ☐

b) I wish everyone would be quiet so we can do the lesson .... ☐

c) Everyone else is mucking about so I will too .... ☐

d) Is there anything I can do to settle the class down? .... ☐

e) If I don't join in the others will have a go at me .... ☐

7. If you have WORKED WELL, which of the following do you like?

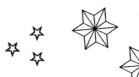

 ✔ TICK as many boxes as you like! ✔

a) A GOOD MARK written in my book .... ☐

b) My work put on DISPLAY with other pupil's work .... ☐

c) The teacher to PRAISE my work TO ME .... ☐

d) The teacher to PRAISE my work TO THE CLASS .... ☐

e) A LETTER HOME about it .... ☐

f) Take it to SHOW TO THE HEADTEACHER .... ☐

g) A STICKER put in my book .... ☐

8. If you could CHOOSE some REWARDS for GOOD WORK and BEHAVIOUR, what would you MOST like them to be?

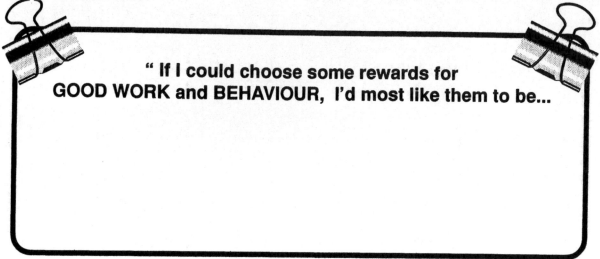

" If I could choose some rewards for GOOD WORK and BEHAVIOUR, I'd most like them to be...

9. What DO YOU THINK your class would NEED TO DO to GET A REWARD?

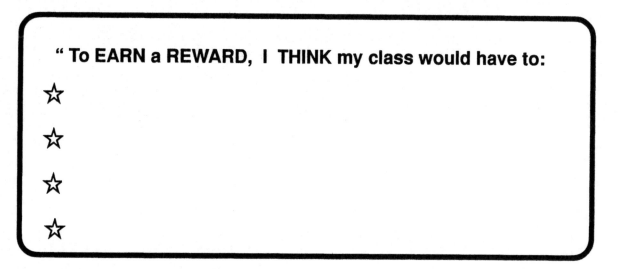

" To EARN a REWARD, I THINK my class would have to:

☆

☆

☆

☆

10. Imagine a NEW PUPIL has come from ANOTHER SCHOOL and is JOINING YOUR CLASS. Try to DESCRIBE the class to them with a few words or in a few sentences.

Eg: Popular with teachers, noisy, unfriendly, friendly, hardworking, get lots of rewards, get told off a lot

I think OUR CLASS is....

11. What could YOU DO to help the new pupil FEEL WELCOME?

> **To help the new pupil feel welcome I could ...**

12. When you have some FREE TIME, for example when you have COMPLETED a PIECE of WORK, would you like the chance to do any of the following?

a) Play a board game of chess or draughts ....

b) Reading a favourite magazine / comic ....

c) Helping to put up posters or displays in your classroom ....

d) Filling in puzzle books ....

e) Doing extra work ....

f) Doing your own work project ....

g) Paper / pens to do drawing etc ....

13. Write down TWO NAMES for EACH of the following questions.

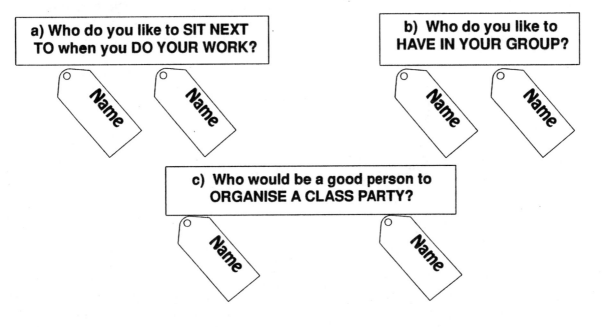

a) Who do you like to SIT NEXT TO when you DO YOUR WORK?

b) Who do you like to HAVE IN YOUR GROUP?

c) Who would be a good person to ORGANISE A CLASS PARTY?

14. WHY do you think your GROUP / CLASS has been CHOSEN for THIS QUESTIONNAIRE?

PUT A CIRCLE around AS MANY of the following suggestions as you want to ....

NOT ENOUGH WORK gets done   **Too much WALKING ABOUT the classroom**

Too much CALLING OUT TO the TEACHER

Too much FIDGETING   **Noisy**   **Too much FIGHTING**

Not very good at LISTENING to EACH OTHER

Too much ARGUING   **Bad at LINING UP**

Not very good at LISTENING to our TEACHER

TOO MUCH TALKING to each other

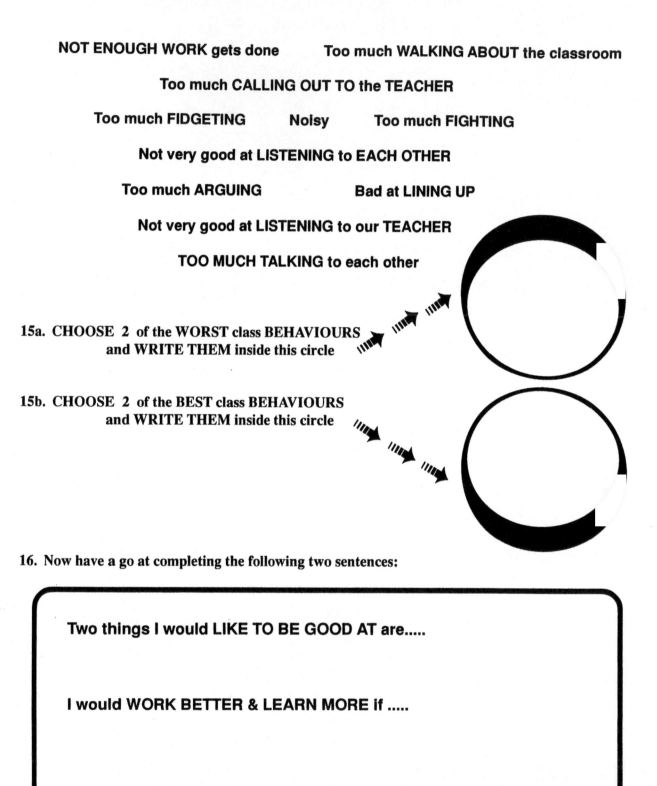

15a. CHOOSE 2 of the WORST class BEHAVIOURS
and WRITE THEM inside this circle

15b. CHOOSE 2 of the BEST class BEHAVIOURS
and WRITE THEM inside this circle

16. Now have a go at completing the following two sentences:

> Two things I would LIKE TO BE GOOD AT are.....
>
>
> I would WORK BETTER & LEARN MORE if .....

THANK YOU for your help in completing this QUESTIONNAIRE.

      From *Classroom Management* – © 1998 Harry Ayers and Francesca Gray – David Fulton Publishers

SECONDARY CLASS / GROUP QUESTIONNAIRE

SCHOOL		DATE	
PUPIL		FORM	

This questionnaire is to help teachers plan work and activities for you. It is a chance for you to say what you think. Please think carefully about your answers and try to complete all of them.
Thank you.

1.   Here is a list of some of your lessons. PUT A CIRCLE around the TWO which you enjoy most:

MATHS   ENGLISH   SCIENCE   GEOGRAPHY   PSHE

HISTORY   DRAMA   ART   D&T   MUSIC

FRENCH   GAMES   HUMANITIES   P.E.   TUTORIAL

RELIGIOUS EDUCATION   WORLD LANGUAGES

2a.   WRITE ONE of the lessons you have put a circle round here: ⑄➡

2b.   WHAT do YOU like about this lesson?   Put a circle around the things you like about it.

The KIND of work   **The AMOUNT of work**   **The LEVEL of work**

The pupils you SIT with   **The pupils you WORK with**

The TEACHER:

   Caring / Friendly / Interesting / Funny / Strict / Fair / Helpful

   Encouraging / Marks our work regularly / Gives us different things to do

2c.   In which lessons do you think your class / group behaves BEST?

3a.   In which lessons do you think your class / group behaves WORST?

3b. What do you think your group / class DISLIKES about some lessons?
Put a circle around the things YOU THINK they dislike.

Not enough DISCUSSION   TOO MUCH reading   Work too HARD

Pupils are NOISY   TOO MUCH discussion   Teacher doesn't EXPLAIN things

Teacher talks for TOO LONG   Too much WRITING   Too much HOMEWORK

DON'T UNDERSTAND the work   Not enough READING   Work is TOO EASY

Students need MORE HELP with work   NOT ENOUGH homework

4. What do you think makes your group/class BEHAVE WELL in different lessons?

✎ Choose 3 subjects in which your group / class is usually well behaved.
Write them in the left hand coloumn.

✔ Tick the things if you think they help your group/class BEHAVE WELL in different lessons.

Things that make our group / class behave well in lessons.

SUBJECTS ✎	Teacher is popular? ✔	Teacher is fair? ✔	Teacher likes us? ✔	Like the subject? ✔	Under-stand the work? ✔	Know how much time we've got to finish work? ✔	Help with home-work? ✔

5. Tick the things you think make your class SETTLE DOWN QUICKLY to work and BEHAVE well.

a) You like the teacher .... ☐
b) You find the work interesting .... ☐
c) You do lots of writing in your book .... ☐
d) You don't have to write anything .... ☐
e) You get lots of help .... ☐
f) You work in groups .... ☐
g) You work on your own .... ☐
h) You know how much work you are expected to do in the lesson .... ☐
i) You are allowed to move freely around in some of the lesson .... ☐
j) You have to stay in your seat throughout the lesson .... ☐

6. When your class is MUCKING ABOUT and the TEACHER IS TRYING TO TEACH the class, how do YOU USUALLY FEEL:

a) This is a good laugh, I'll join in .... ☐
b) I wish everyone would be quiet so we can do the lesson .... ☐
c) Everyone else is mucking about so I will too .... ☐
d) Is there anything I can do to settle the class down? .... ☐
e) If I don't join in the others will have a go at me .... ☐

7. If you have WORKED WELL, which of the following do you like?

✔ Tick as many boxes as you like! ✔

a) A good mark written in my book .... ☐
b) My work put on display with other pupil's work .... ☐
c) The teacher to praise my work to me .... ☐
d) The teacher to praise my work to the class .... ☐
e) A letter home about it .... ☐
f) Take it to show to the Headteacher .... ☐
g) Take it to show to the Year Head .... ☐

h) Anything else? Please write it in the box below:

8. If you could CHOOSE some REWARDS for GOOD WORK and BEHAVIOUR, what would you MOST like them to be?

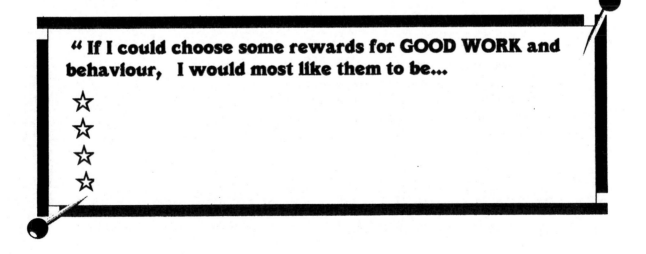

" If I could choose some rewards for GOOD WORK and behaviour, I would most like them to be...

☆
☆
☆
☆

9. **What DO YOU THINK your class would need to do to GET A REWARD?**

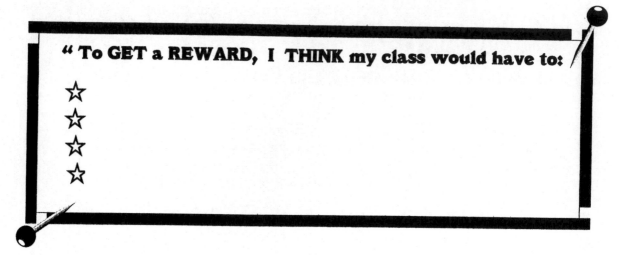

" To GET a REWARD, I THINK my class would have to:

☆

☆

☆

☆

10. **Imagine a NEW PUPIL has come from ANOTHER SCHOOL and is JOINING YOUR CLASS. Try to DESCRIBE the class to them with a few words or in a few sentences.**

Eg: Noisy, unfriendly, friendly, hardworking, get lots of rewards, get lots of detentions...

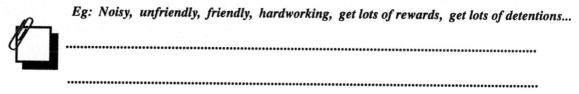

....

....

....

....

11. **What could YOU DO to make the new pupil FEEL WELCOME?**

....

....

....

12. **When you have some FREE TIME, for example when you have COMPLETED a PIECE of WORK, would you like the chance to do any of the following?**

a) **Playing a board game of chess or draughts** .... ☐
b) **Reading a favourite magazine / comic** .... ☐
c) **Helping to put up posters or displays in your tutor room** .... ☐
d) **Filling in puzzle books** .... ☐
e) **Doing extra work** .... ☐
f) **Doing your own work project** .... ☐
g) **Paper / pens to do drawing etc.**.. ☐
h) **Anything other ideas of your own? Please write them in the box below.**

From *Classroom Management* – © 1998 Harry Ayers and Francesca Gray – David Fulton Publishers

13. Write down TWO NAMES for EACH QUESTION.

a) Who do you like to SIT NEXT to when you DO YOUR WORK?

b) Who do you like to HAVE IN YOUR GROUP?

c) Who would be a good person to ORGANISE A CLASS PARTY?

14. Why do you think your class has been chosen for this questionnaire?

....

....

15. What kind of misbehaviours do they show as a class?

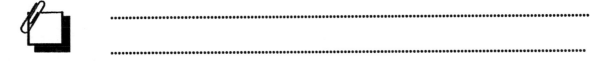

....

....

16. Complete the following two sentences:

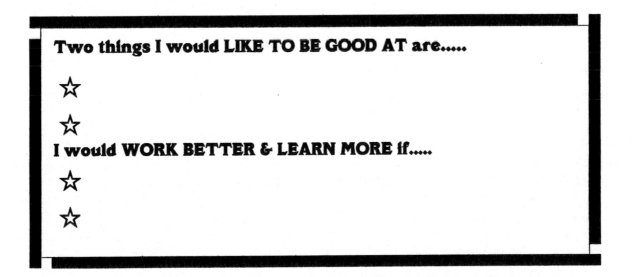

Two things I would LIKE TO BE GOOD AT are.....

☆

☆

I would WORK BETTER & LEARN MORE if.....

☆

☆

THANK YOU FOR YOUR HELP IN COMPLETING THIS QUESTIONNAIRE.

CLASSROOM DISCIPLINE PLAN

This form can be used as a STRUCTURE to enable teachers to FORMULATE a class discipline PLAN.

CLASS/GROUP/FORM:	TEACHER:	NC YEAR:

DESCRIPTION OF CLASS OR FORM'S PROBLEMS:

e.g. high noise levels, low output of work, poor quality of work, wandering around the room, distracting or interfering with others, chatting to each other, fidgeting, reluctance to start work or finish work.

TIMES, LATENCY, FREQUENCY, DURATION AND SEVERITY OF PROBLEMS:

Problems occur: *Mondays, Tuesdays, Wednesdays, Thursdays, Fridays. Mornings - Afternoons*

Problems occur   *Immediately, after a short time, in the middle of lessons, towards the end of lessons, at the end of lessons.*

Problems occur: *In all lessons, in most lessons, in some lessons.*

Problems last: *All the time, most of the time, some of the time.*

Problems are: *Severe, moderate, mild.*

PROBLEMS OCCURRING DURING PARTICULAR ACTIVITIES:

Problems occur during: *e.g. reading, writing, story telling, mathematics, creative, games.*

    From *Classroom Management* – © 1998 Harry Ayers and Francesca Gray – David Fulton Publishers

CLASS TARGETS (SMART):

1.

2.

3.

4.

SUCCESS CRITERIA:

1.

2.

3.

4.

CLASS INTERVENTIONS:

e.g. positive reinforcement programme, class detention, class report, rearrangement of groups or forms, rearrangement of seating, changing classroom environment, moving pupil (s) to different option(s) / class / form, changing teaching style / methods / materials, differentiating lessons, class contract, class conferencing, contacting and involving parents carers:

EVALUATION:

e.g. problems disappeared, been reduced, remain as before, become intermittent, become rare:

Bibliography

Ausubel, D. P. (1963) *The Psychology of Meaningful Verbal Learning*. New York: Grune & Stratton.

Ayers, H., Clarke, D., Murray, A. (1995) *Perspectives on Behaviour*. London: David Fulton Publishers.

Badger, B. (1985) 'Behavioural problems – some cautionary notes', *Maladjustment and Therapeutic Education* **3**(2), 4–11.

Bandura, A. (1977) *Social Learning Theory*. Englewood Cliffs, NJ: Prentice-Hall.

Bandura, A. (1986) *Social Foundations of Thought and Action*. Englewood Cliffs, NJ: Prentice-Hall.

Beck, A. T. (1970) 'Cognitive therapy: nature and relation to behavior therapy', *Behavior Therapy* **1**, 184–200.

Beck, A. T. (1976) *Cognitive Therapy and the Emotional Disorders*. New York: International Universities Press.

Bem, D. J. (1972) 'Self-perception theory', in Berkowitz, L. (ed.) *Advances in Experimental Social Psychology*, Vol. 6, 1–62. New York: Academic Press.

Bruner, J. S., Goodknow, J. J., Austin, G. A. (1956) *A Study of Thinking*. New York: Wiley.

Canter, L. and Canter, M. (1992) *Assertive Discipline: Positive Behavior Management for Today's Classroom*, 2nd edn. Santa Monica, CA: Canter Associates.

Charles, C. M. (1996) *Building Classroom Discipline*, 5th edn. New York: Longman.

Cooper, P., Smith, C. J., Upton, G. (1994) *Emotional and Behavioural Difficulties*. London: Routledge.

Craighead, L. W., Craighead, W. E., Kazdin, A. E., Mahoney, M. J. (1994) *Cognitive and Behavioral Interventions*. Needham Heights: Allyn & Bacon.

Creemers, B. P. M. (1994) *The Effective Classroom*. London: Cassell.

DES (1978) *Special Educational Needs: The Warnock Report*. London: HMSO.

DES (1989) *The Elton Report*. London: HMSO.

DfEE (1994) *Code of Practice on the Identification and Assessment of Special Needs*. London. Department for Education.

Dreikurs, R. (1968) *Psychology in the Classroom*, 2nd edn. New York: Harper & Row.

D'Zurilla, T. J. (1986) *Problem-Solving Therapy*. New York: Springer.

D'Zurilla, T. J. and Goldfried, M. R. (1971) 'Problem solving and behaviour modification', *Journal of Abnormal Psychology*.

Ellis, A. (1962) *Reason and Emotion in Psychotherapy*. New York: Lyle Stuart.

Ellis, A. (1977) 'The basic clinical theory of rational-emotive therapy', in Ellis, A. and Grieger, R. (eds) *Handbook of Rational-Emotive Therapy*, 3–34. New York: Springer.

Ellis, A. (1979) 'The theory of rational-emotive therapy', in Ellis, A. and Whiteley, J. M. (eds) *Theoretical and Empirical Foundations of Rational-Emotive Therapy*, 33–60. Monterey: Brooks/Cole.

Farrell, P. (1997) *Teaching Pupils with Learning Difficulties: Strategies and Solutions*. London: Cassell.

Ginott, H. (1971) *Teacher and Child*. New York: Macmillan.

Goodman, R. and Scott, S. (1997) *Child Psychiatry*. Oxford: Blackwell Science.

Gordon, T. (1989) *Discipline that Works: Promoting Self-Discipline in Children*. New York: Random House.

Hallam, S. and Toutounji, I. (1996) *What Do We Know About the Grouping of Pupils by Ability?* London: University of London, Institute of Education.

Hargreaves, D. H., Hestor, K. H., Mellor, J. M. (1975) *Deviance in Classrooms*. London: Routledge & Kegan Paul.

Herbert, M. (1991) *Clinical Child Psychology*. Chichester: Wiley.

Jones, R. A. (1995) *The Child–School Interface*. London: Cassell.

Kazdin, A. E. (1994) *Behavior Modification in Applied Settings*, 5th edn. Pacific Grove, CA: Brooks/Cole.

Kounin, J. (1977) *Discipline and Group Management in Classrooms*, rev. edn. New York: Holt, Reinhart & Winston.

Kyriacou, C. (1997) *Effective Teaching in Schools*, 2nd edn. Cheltenham: Stanley Thornes (Publishers) Ltd.

Martin, J. and Sugarman, J. (1993) *Models of Classroom Management*, 2nd edn. Bellingham: Detselig Enterprises Ltd, Calgary and Temeron Books Inc.

McManus, M. (1990) *Troublesome Behaviour in the Classroom*, 2nd edn. London: Routledge.

Meichenbaum, D. and Asarnow, J. (1979) 'Cognitive-behavioral modification and metacognitive development: Implications for the classroom', in Kendall, P. C. and Hollon, S. D. (eds) *Cognitive-Behavioral Interventions: Theory, Research and Procedures*, 11–35. New York: Academic Press.

Meichenbaum, D., Rowland, S., Gruesen, L., Cameron, R. (1985) 'Metacognitive assessment', in Yussen, S. (ed.) *The Growth of Reflection in Children*. Orlando: Academic Press.

Mercer, C. D. and Mercer, A. R. (1993) *Teaching Students with Learning Problems*, 4th edn. New York: Maxwell-Macmillan.

Molnar, A. and Lindquist, B. (1989) *Changing Problem Behavior in Schools*. San Francisco: Josey Bass.

Moos, R. H. (1979) *Evaluating Educational Environment*. San Francisco: Josey Bass.

Mortimore, P., Sammons, P., Ecob, R., Stoll, L., Lewis, D. (1988) *School Matters: The Junior Years*. Salisbury: Open Books.

Nicolson, D. and Ayers, H. (1995) *Individual Counselling*. London: David Fulton Publishers.

Nicolson, D. and Ayers, H. (1997) *Adolescent Problems*. London: David Fulton Publishers.

Norwich, B. (1990) *Reappraising Special Needs Education*. London: Cassell.

Pavlov, I. P. (1927) *Conditioned Reflexes*. London: Oxford University Press.

Pumfrey, P. D. and Reason, R. (1991) *Specific Learning Difficulties – (Dyslexia) – Challenges and Responses*. London: Routledge.

Reynolds, D. (ed.) (1985) *Studying School Effectiveness*. Lewes: Falmer Press.

Roffey, S. and O'Reirdan, T. (1997) *Infant Classroom Behaviour*. London: David Fulton Publishers.

Rogers, B. (1990) *You Know the Fair Rule*. Harlow: Longman.

Rogers, C. (1969) *The Freedom to Learn*. Columbus, OH: Charles E. Merrill.

Rogers, C. R. (1951) *Client-Centered Therapy*. Boston: Houghton Mifflin.

Rogers, W. (1990) *Supporting Teachers in the Workplace*. Queensland: Jacaranda Press.

Rosenthal, R. and Jacobsen, L. (1968) *Pygmalion in the Classroom*. New York: Holt, Reinhart & Winston.

Rotter, J. B. (1966) 'Generalized expectancies for internal versus external control of reinforcement', *Psychological Monographs* **80**, 1, 609).

Rotter, J. B. (1971) 'External control and internal control', *Psychology Today* **5**, 37–41, 58–9.

Rutter, M., Maughan, B., Mortimore, P., Ouston, J. (1979) *Fifteen Thousand Hours: Secondary Schools and Their Effects on Children*. London: Open Books.

Seligman, M. E. P., Abramson, L. Y., Samuel, A., Von Baeyer, C. (1979) 'Depressive attributional style', *Journal of Abnormal Psychology* **88**, 242–7.

Skinner, B. F. (1953) *Science and Human Behavior*. New York: Macmillan.

Vygotsky, V. (1962) *Thought and Language*. Cambridge, MA: MIT Press.

Watson, J. B. and Raynor, R. (1920) 'Conditional emotional reaction', *Journal of Experimental Psychology*.

Weiner, B. (1988) 'Attribution theory and attributional therapy: Some theoretical observations and suggestions', *British Journal of Clinical Psychology* **27**, 93-104.

Woolfolk, A. E. (1995) *Educational Psychology*, 6th edn. Needham Heights: Allyn & Bacon.

Printed in the United Kingdom
by Lightning Source UK Ltd.
108068UKS00001B/309-330